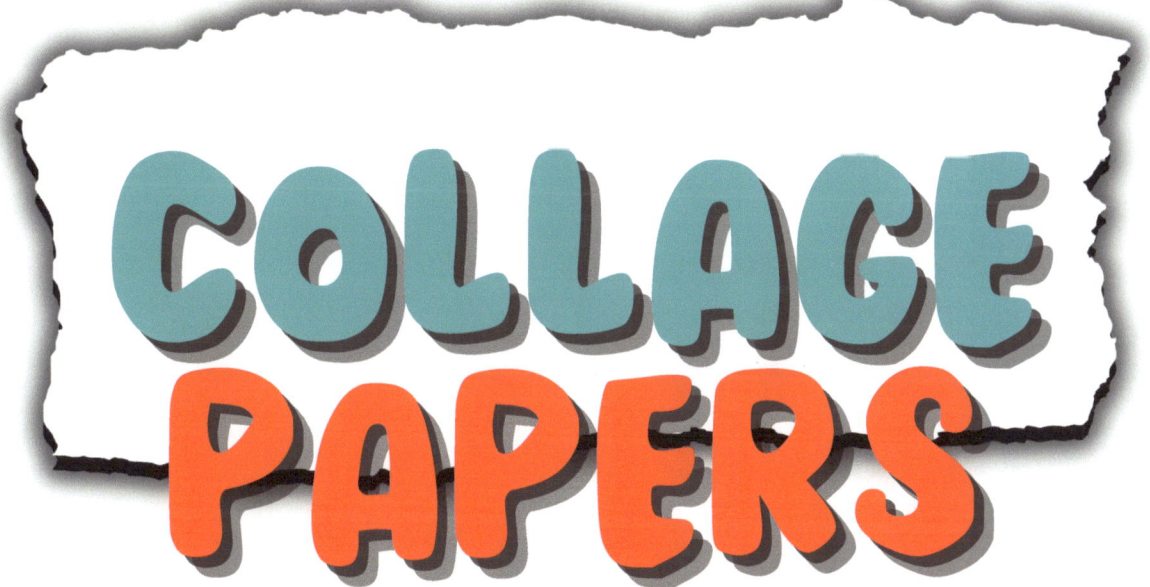

COLLAGE PAPERS

ABSTRACT, ART DECO, RETRO PATTERNS & FACES

Copyright © 2024 Amoo B
ISBN: 9798332680502

Welcome to **Collage Papers Abstract, Art Deco, Retro Patterns and Faces**. This book is a vibrant canvas for artists, crafters, and enthusiasts who cherish the creative process.

How to Use This Book:

Creative Collages: Use these retro patterns and faces to craft stunning collages. Mix and match elements to create your unique compositions, adding a touch of vibrant elegance to your projects.

Scrapbooking: Enhance your scrapbooks with these designs. Each page offers a rich tapestry of colours and shapes, perfect for framing memories in a stylish, creatve way.

DIY Projects: From greeting cards to home décor, these patterns provide endless possibilities. Cut, layer, and arrange the elements to bring a flair flair to your DIY creations.

Inspiration: Let the eclectic mix of designs inspire your next masterpiece. Use the patterns as a muse for paintings, digital art, or mixed media projects.

Follow us on Amazon if you want to be notified of our next project and please do leave a rating of your experience with this book so we can continue to improve our work.

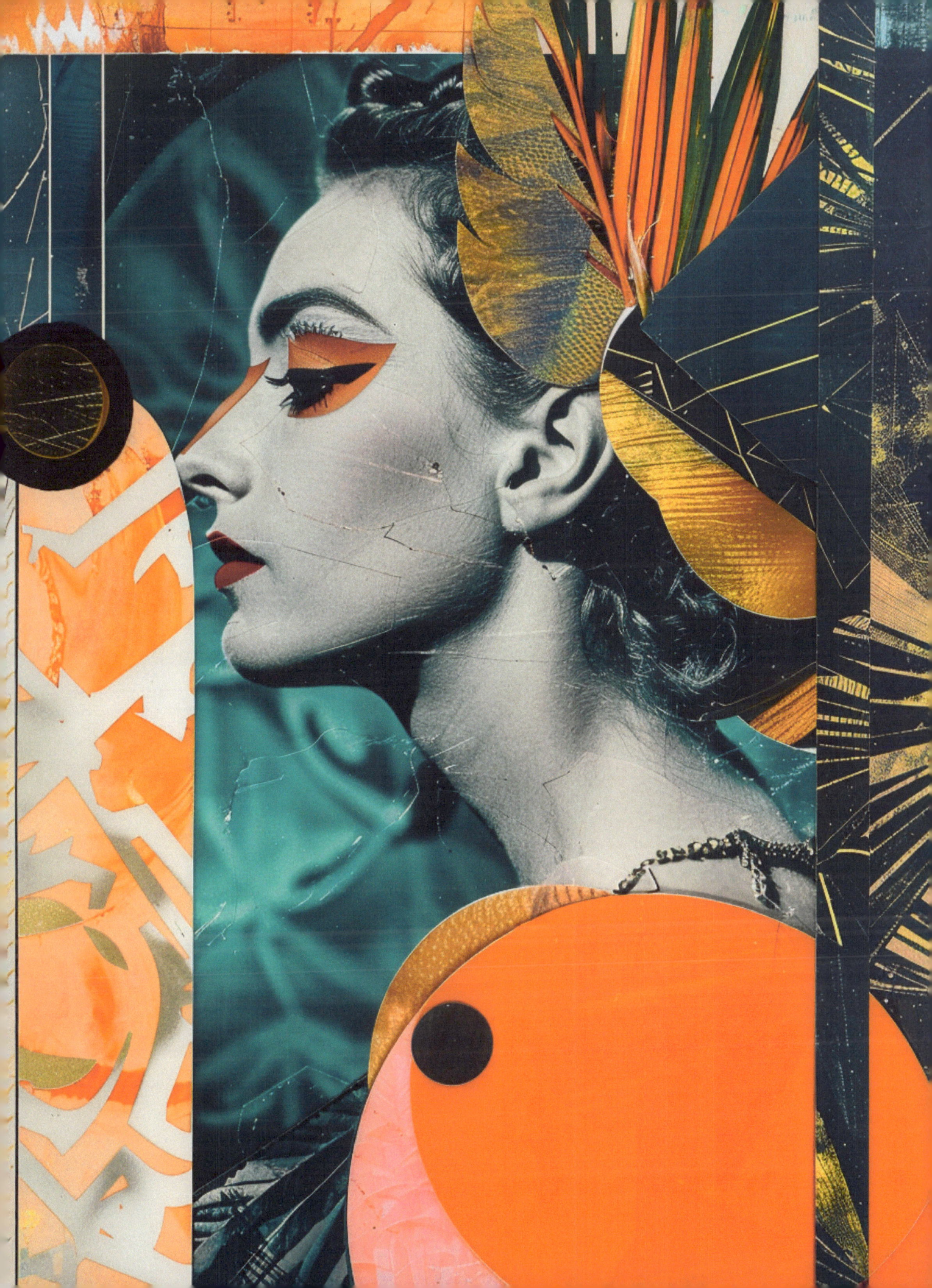

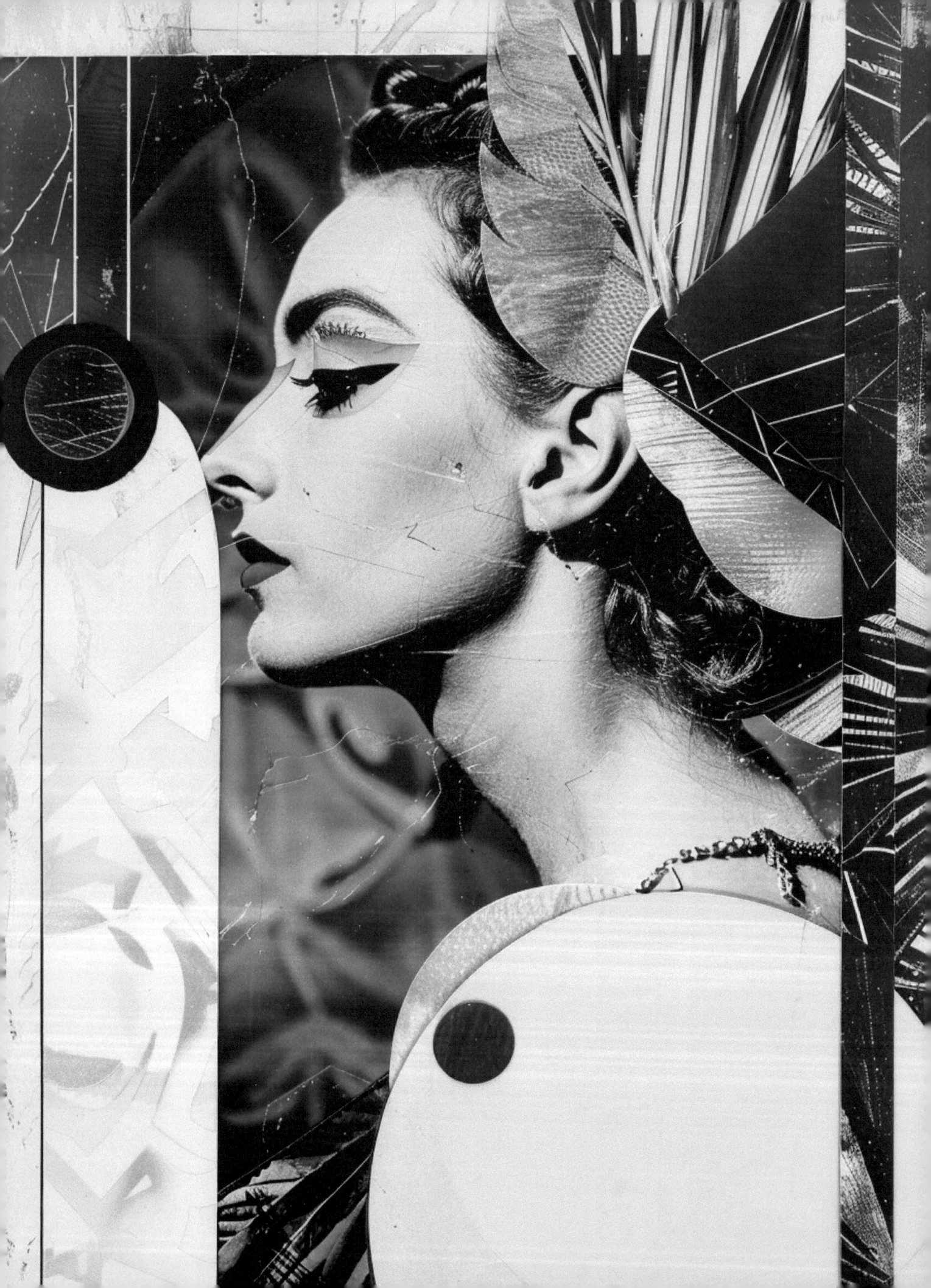

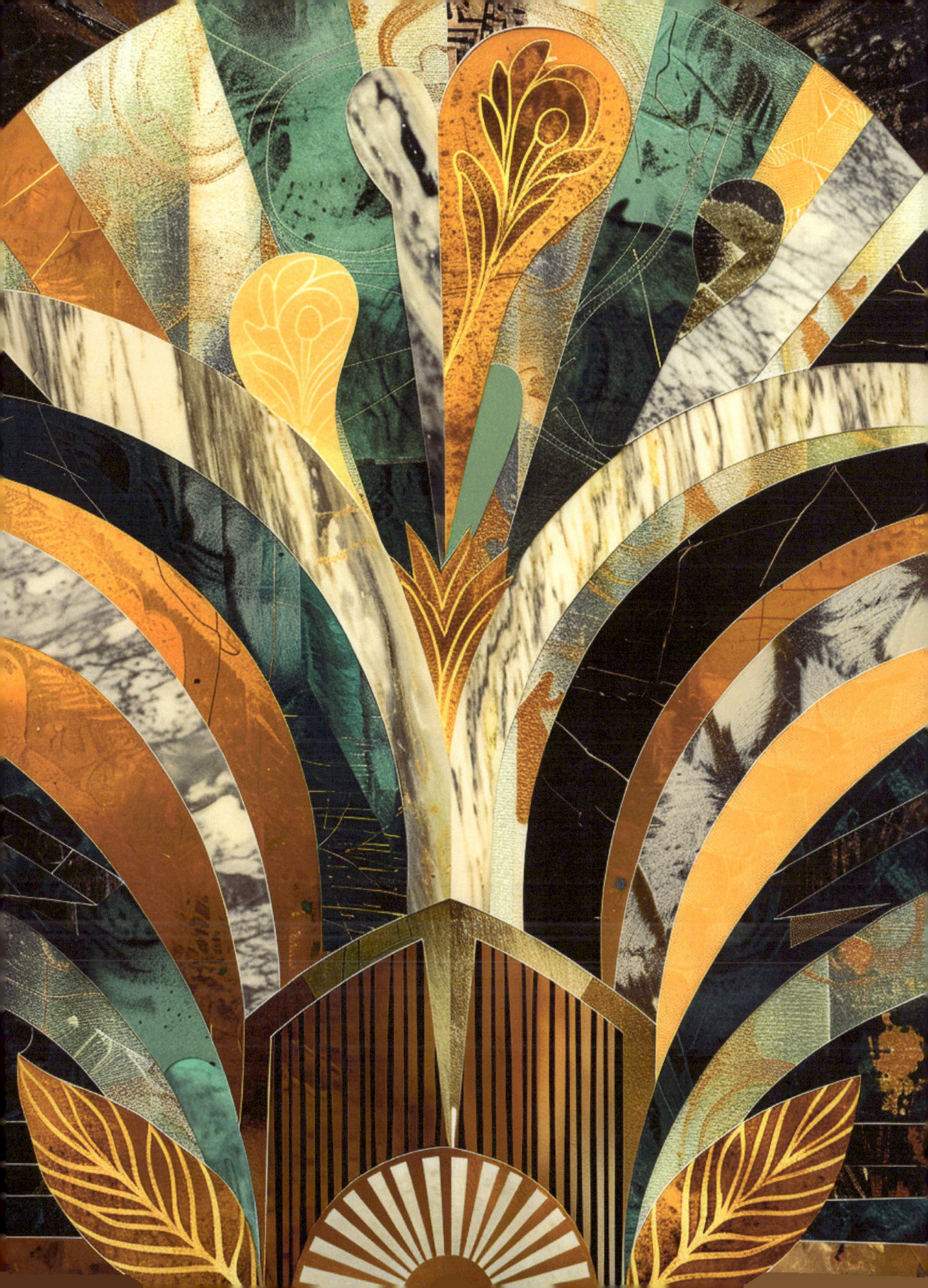

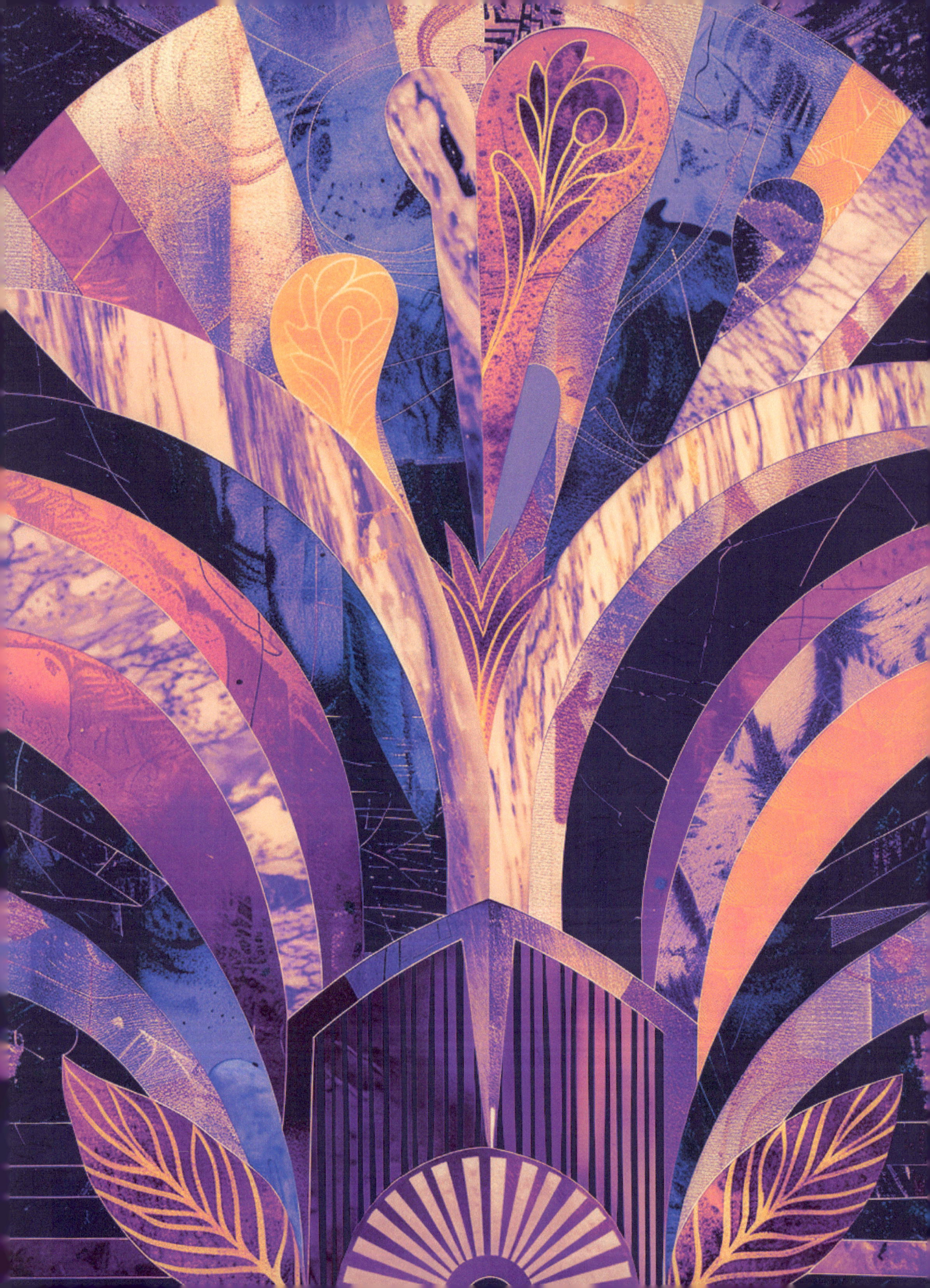

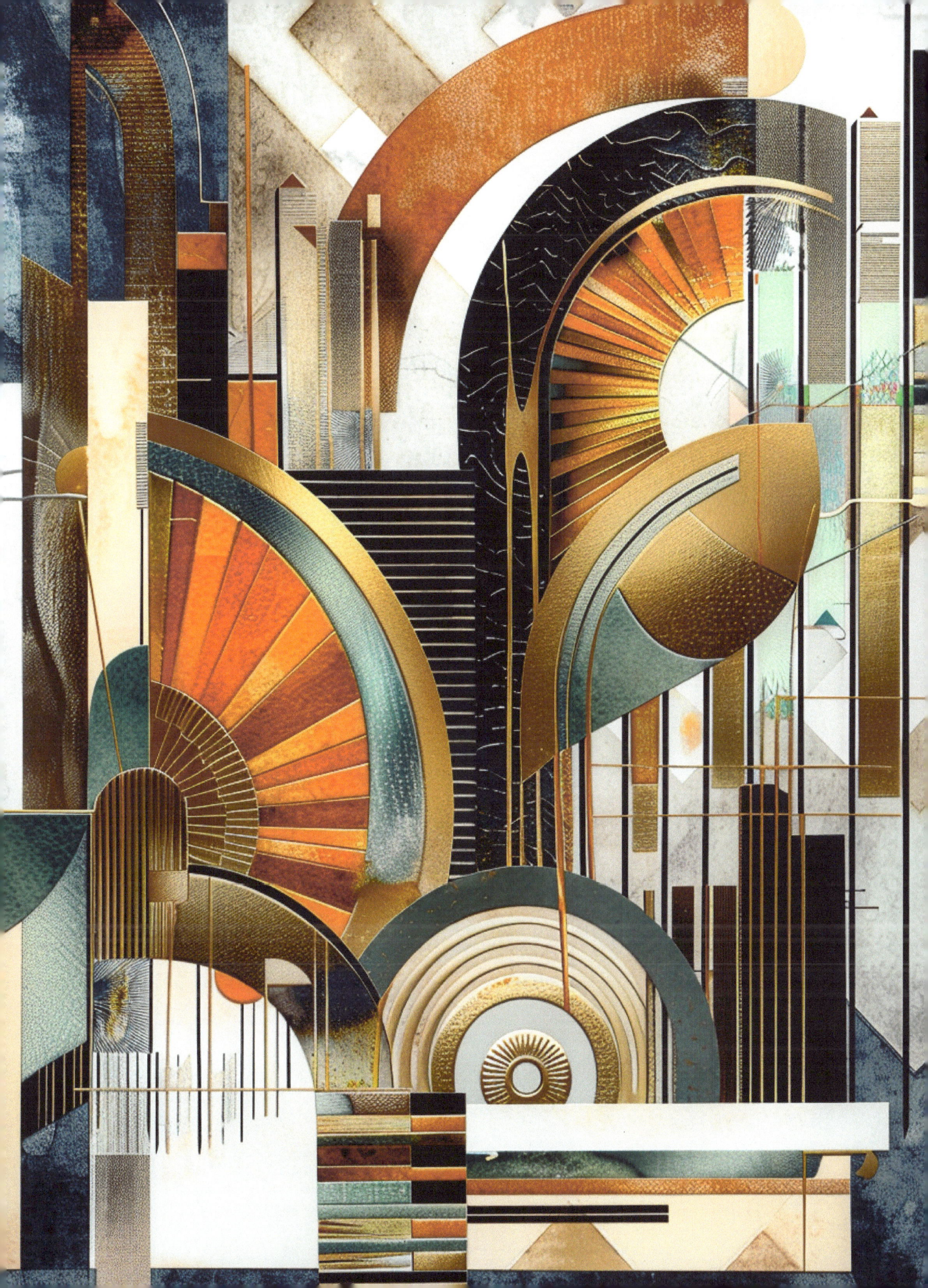

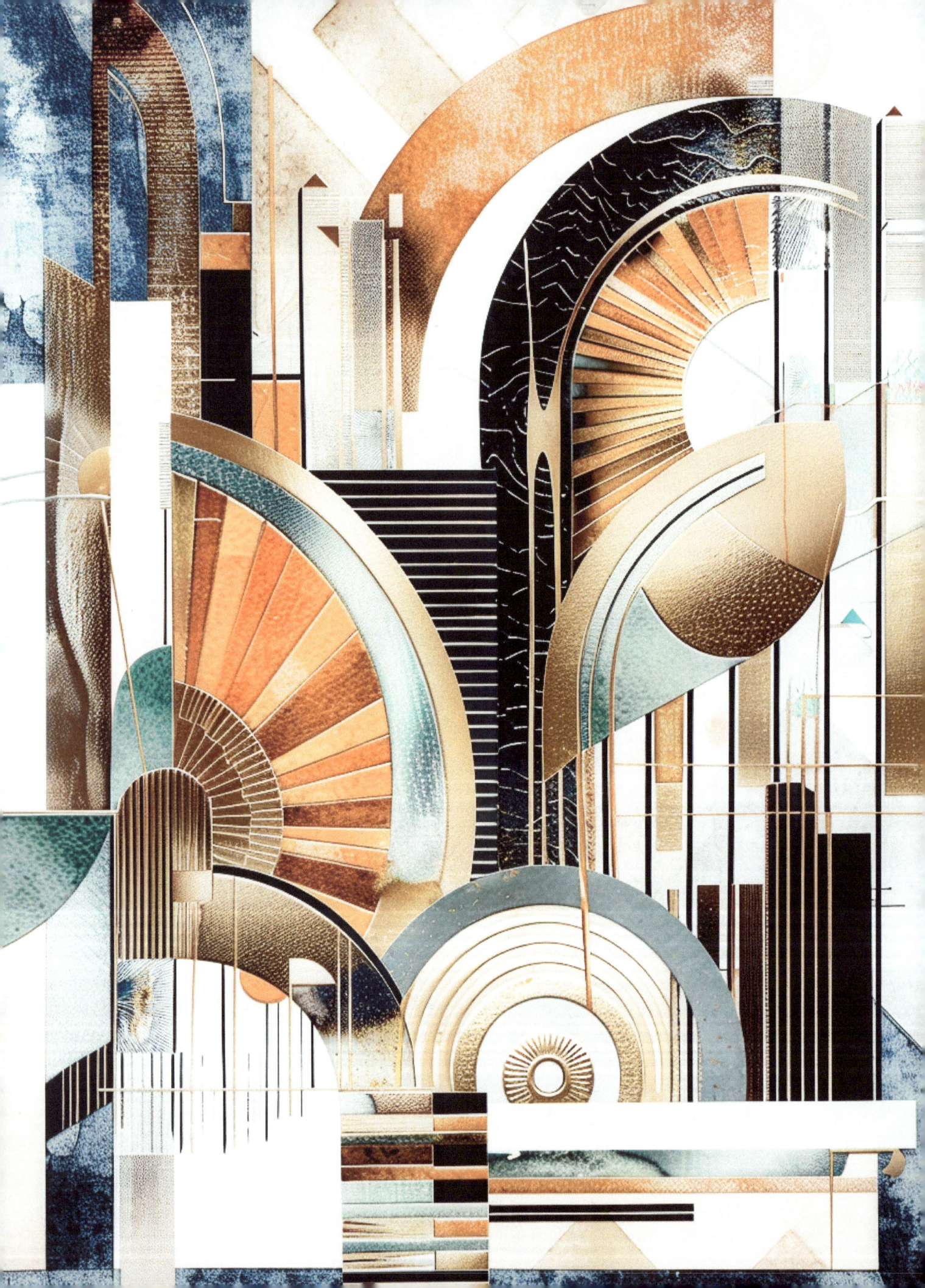

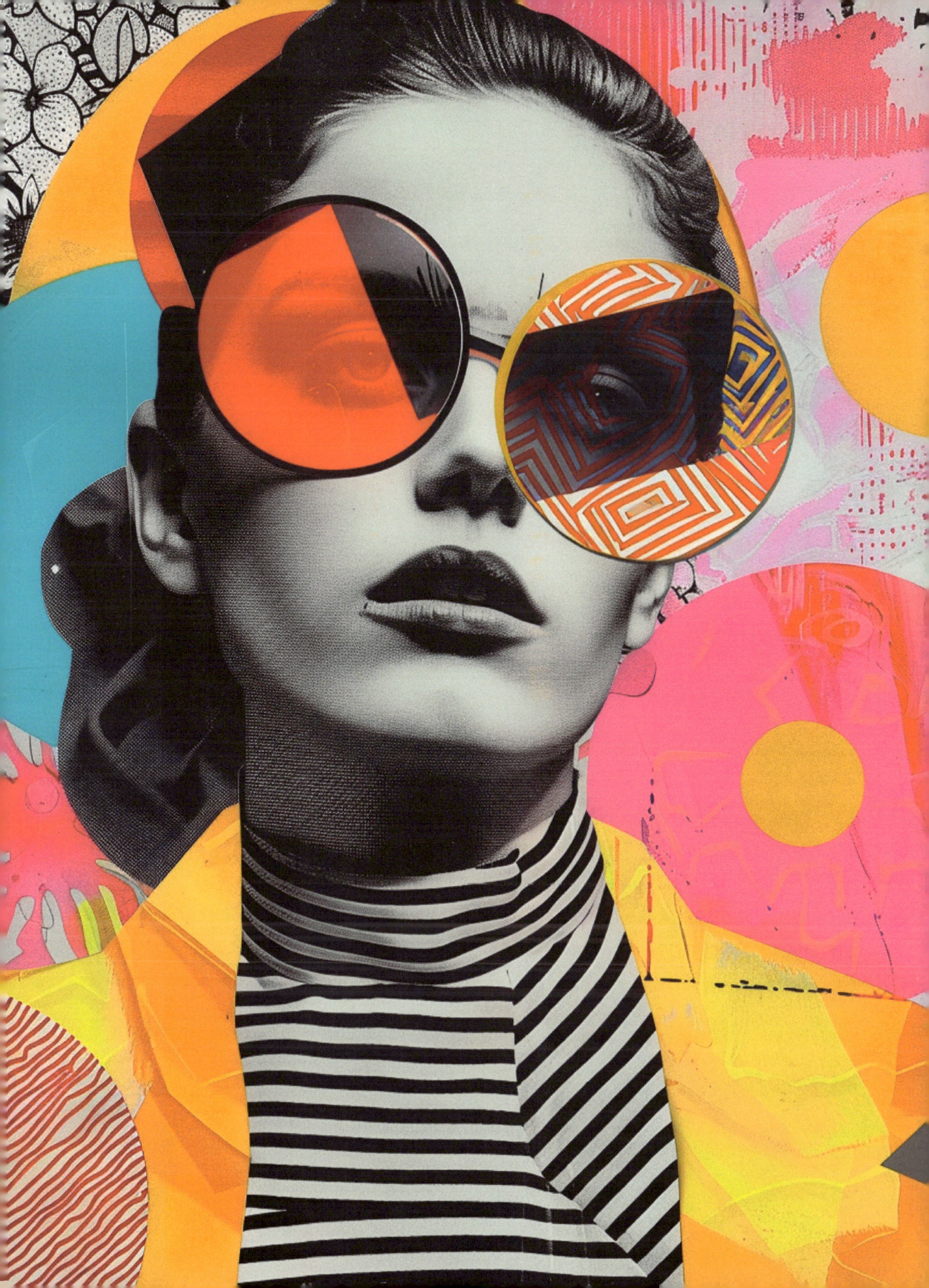

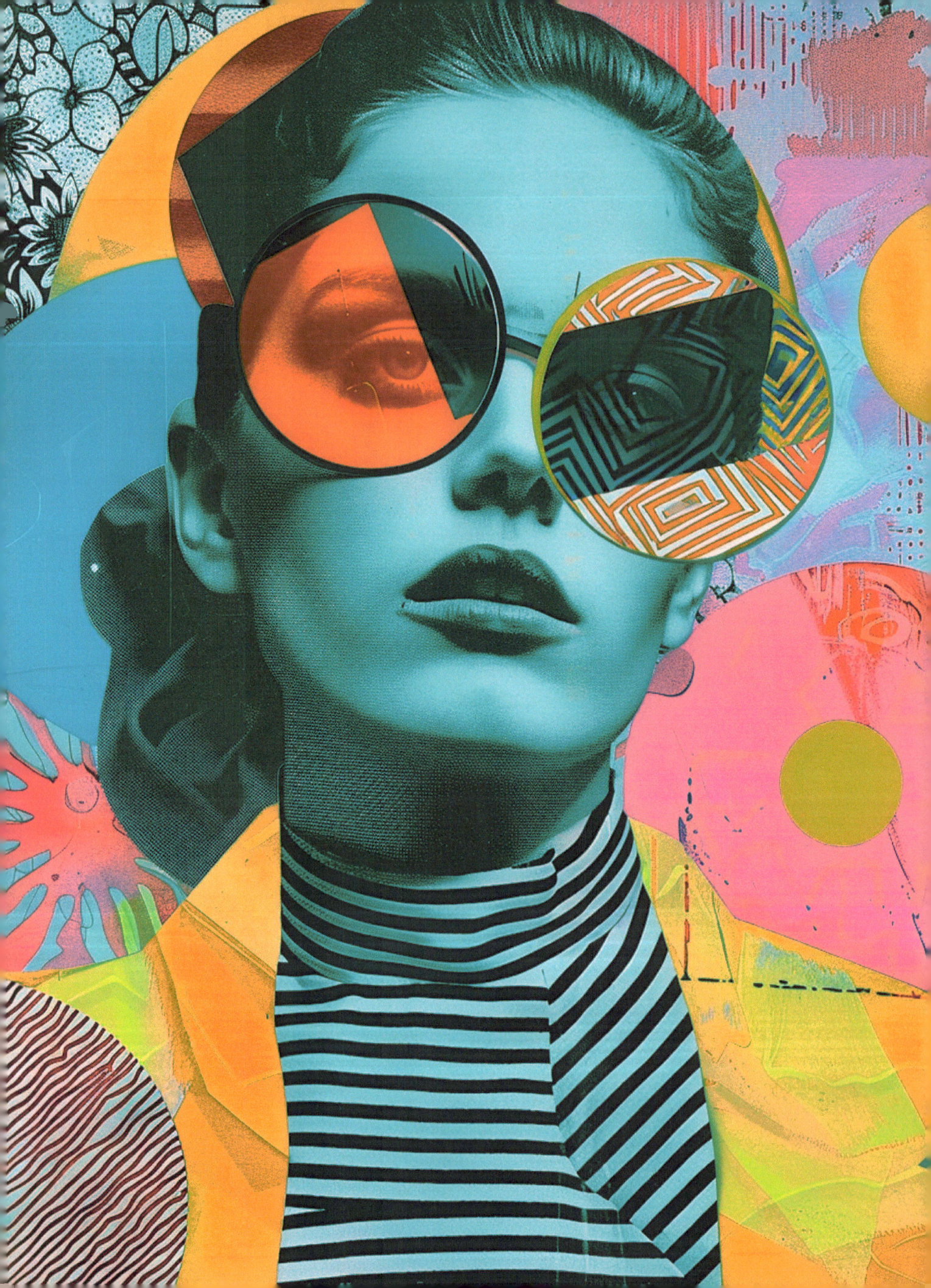

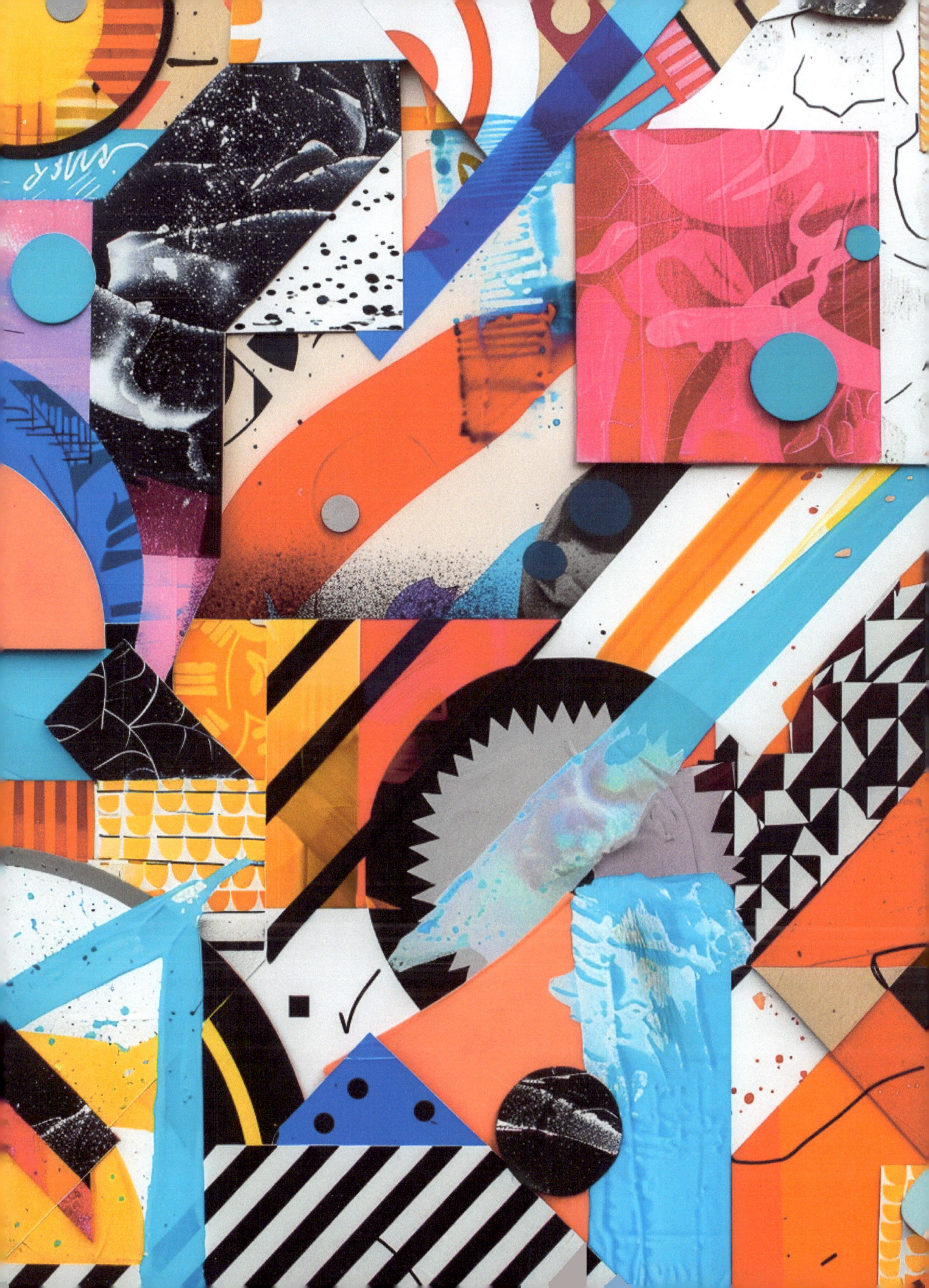

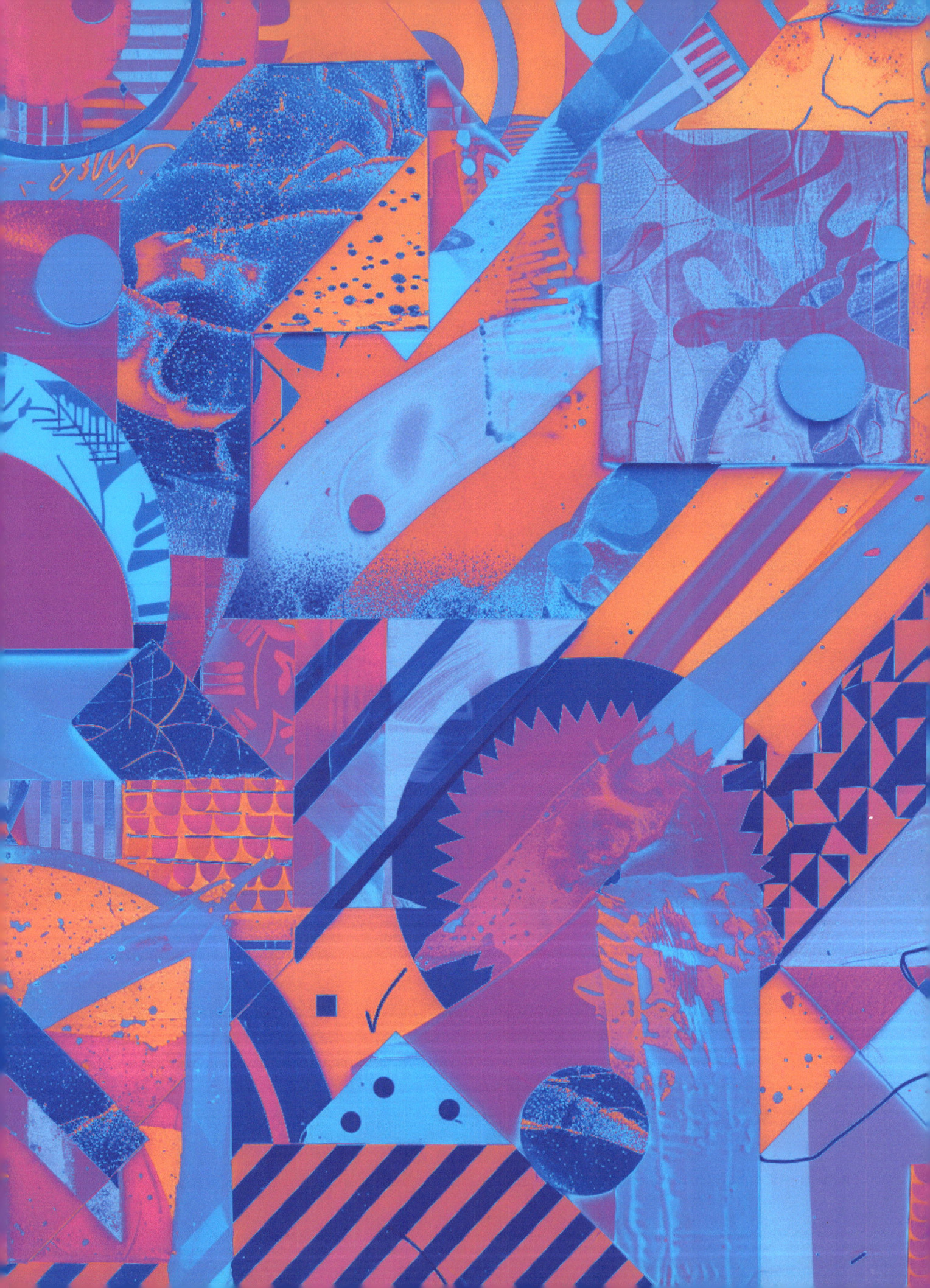

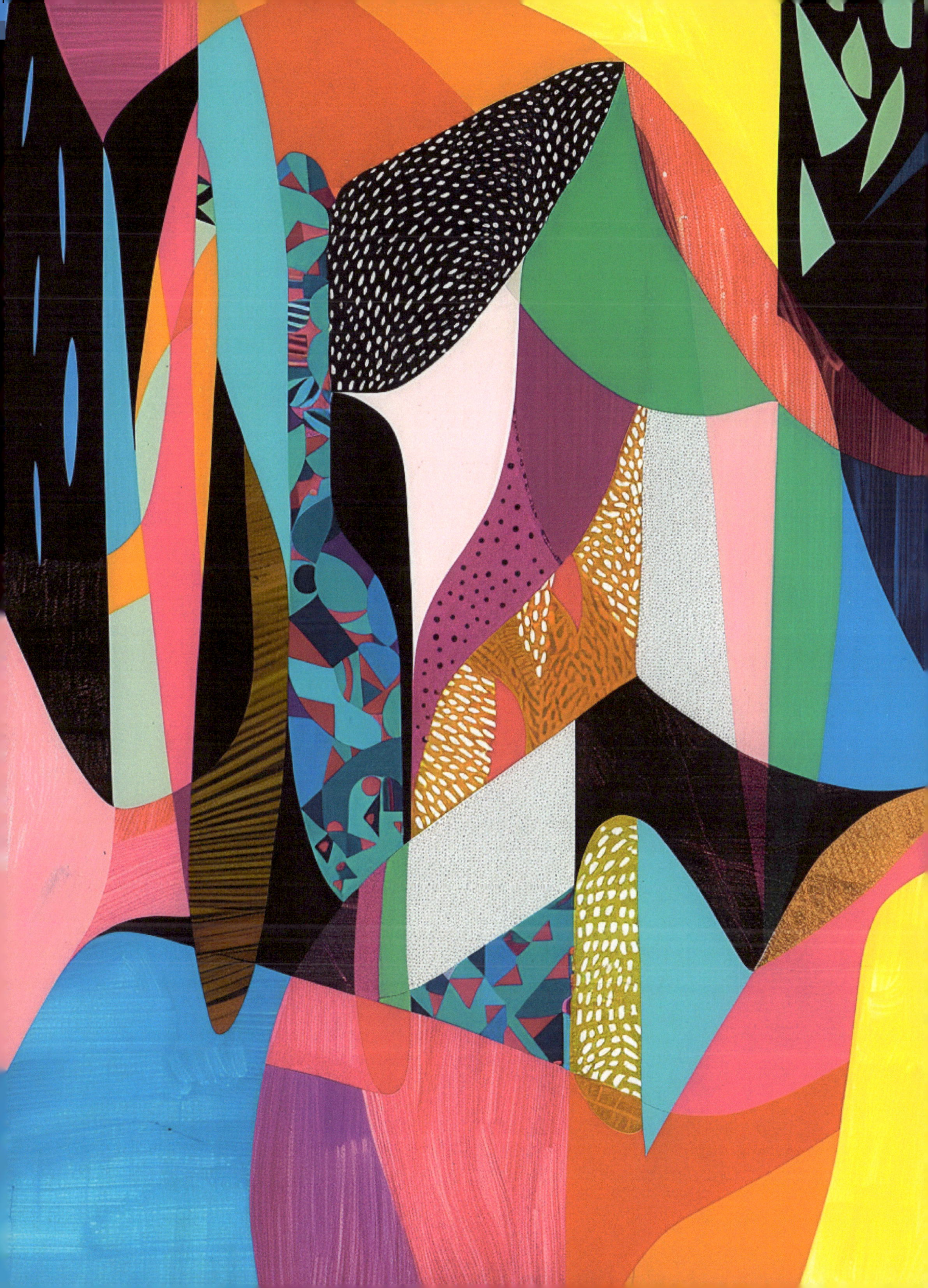

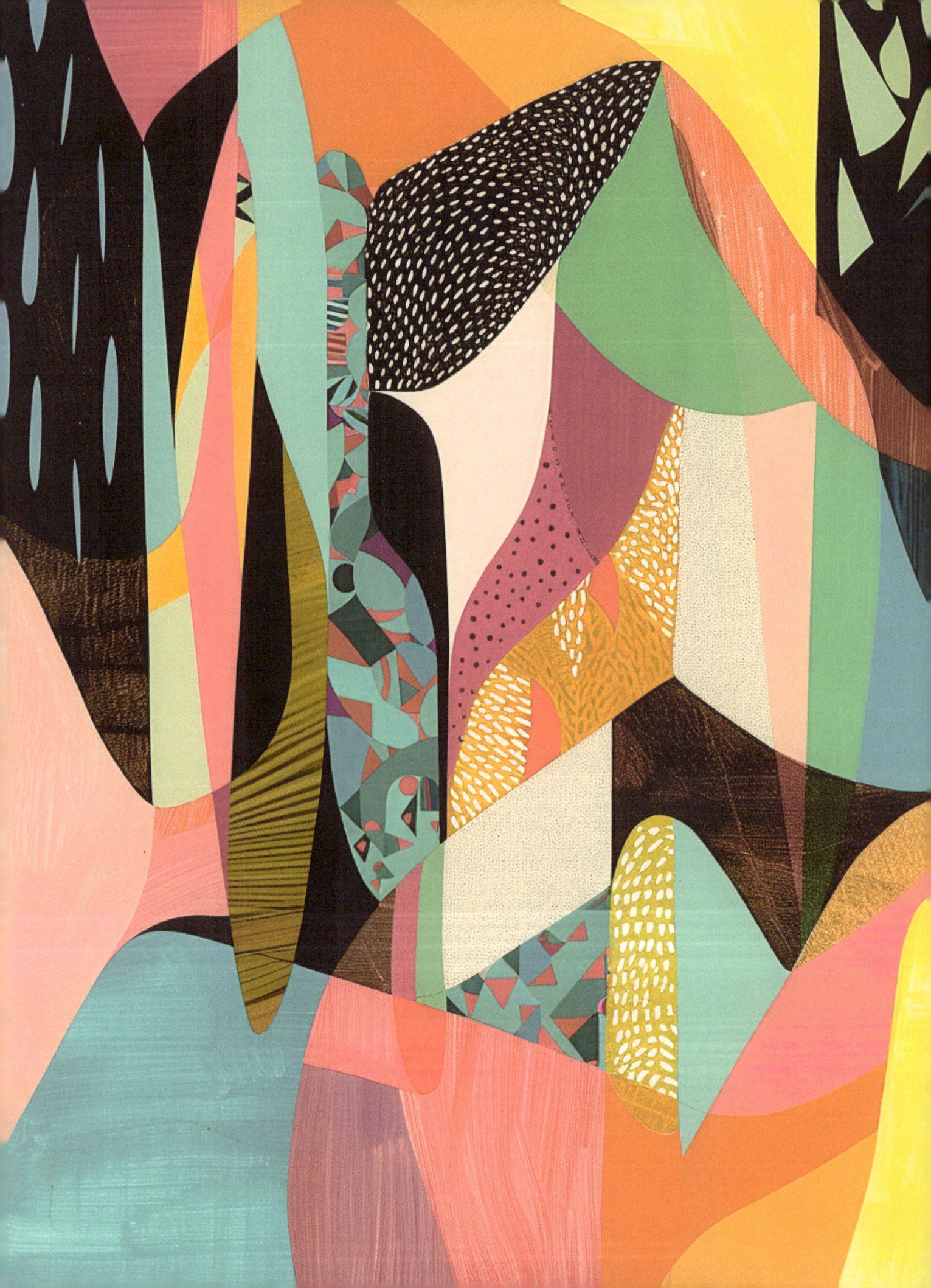

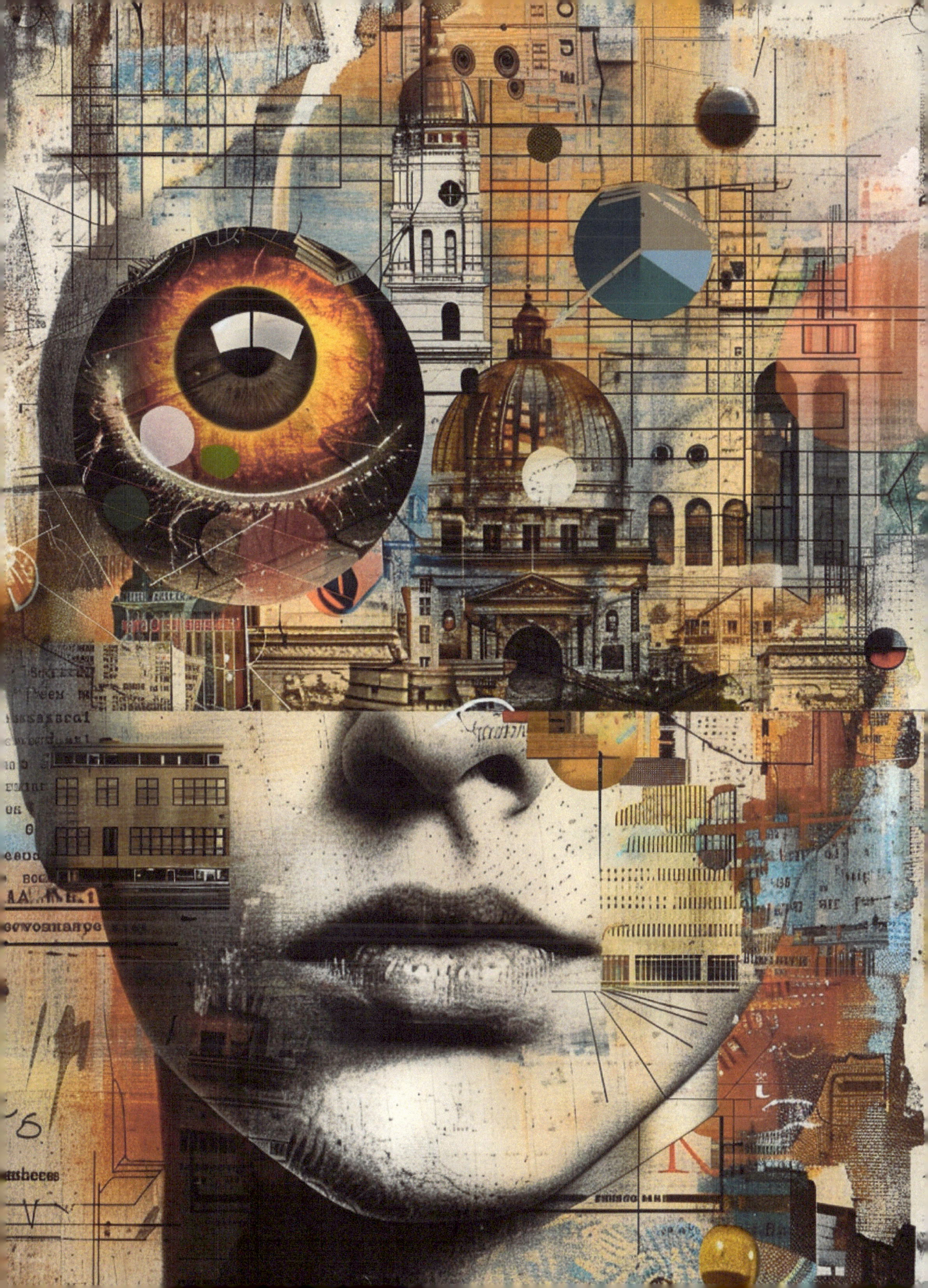

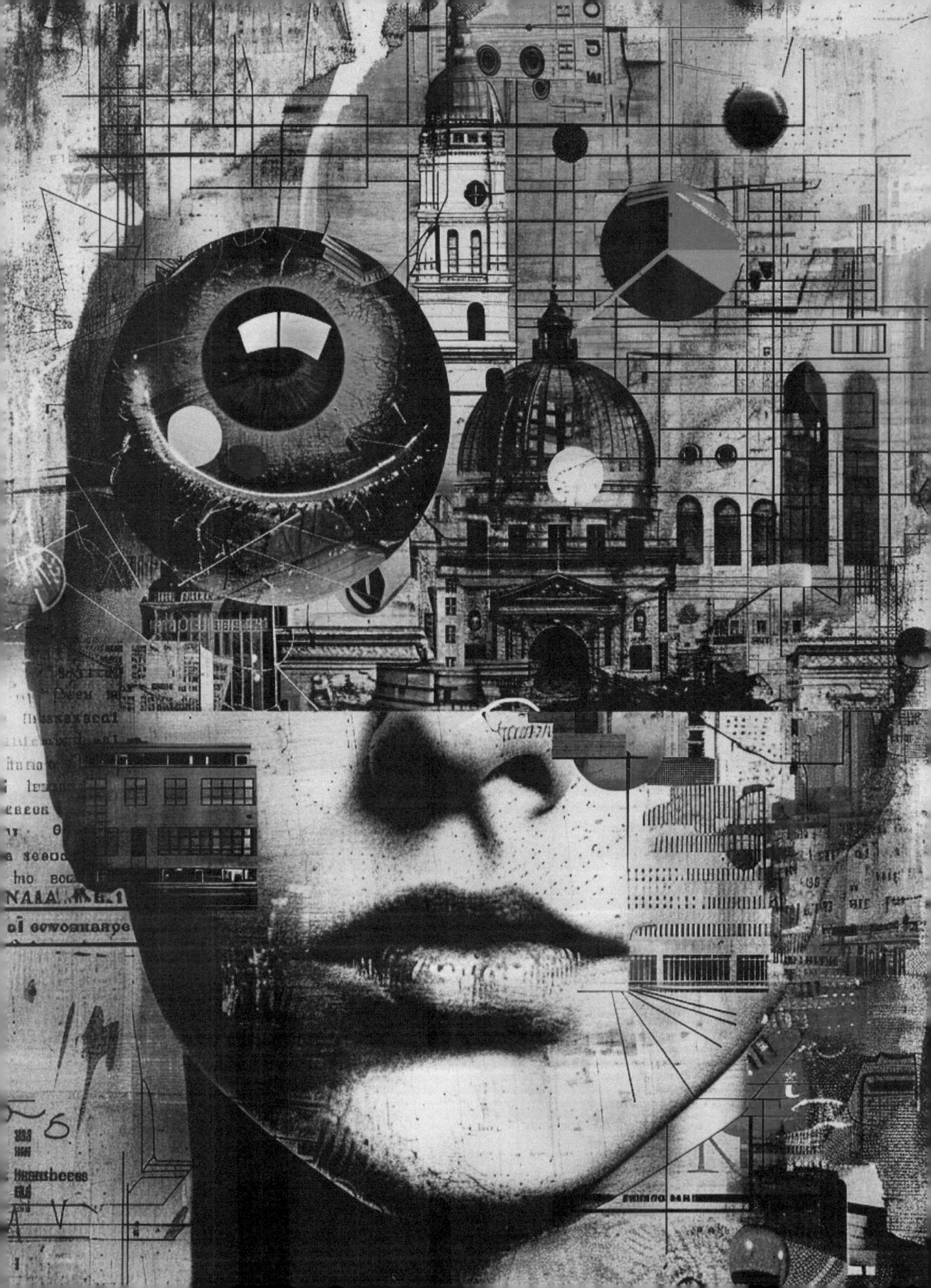

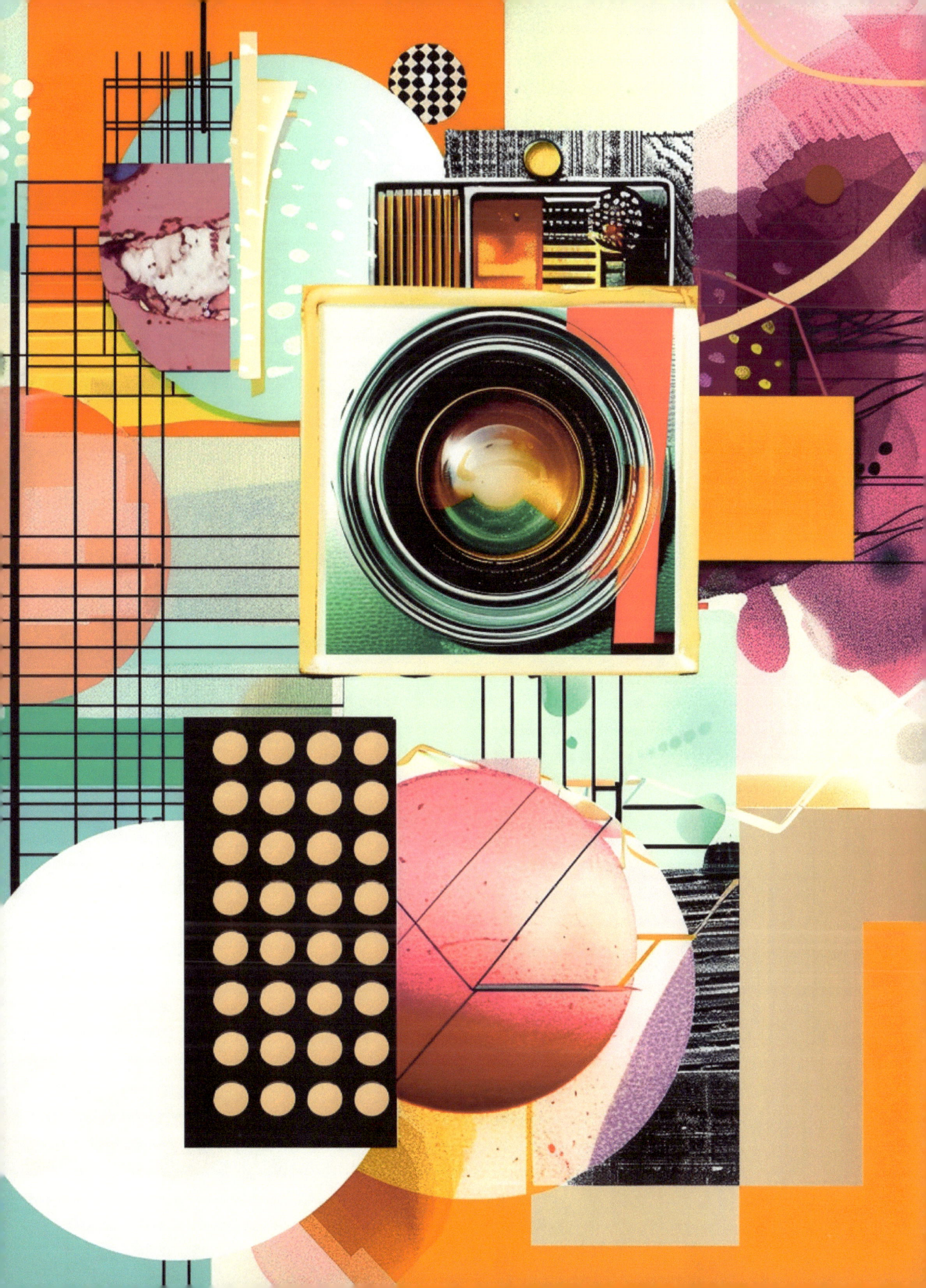

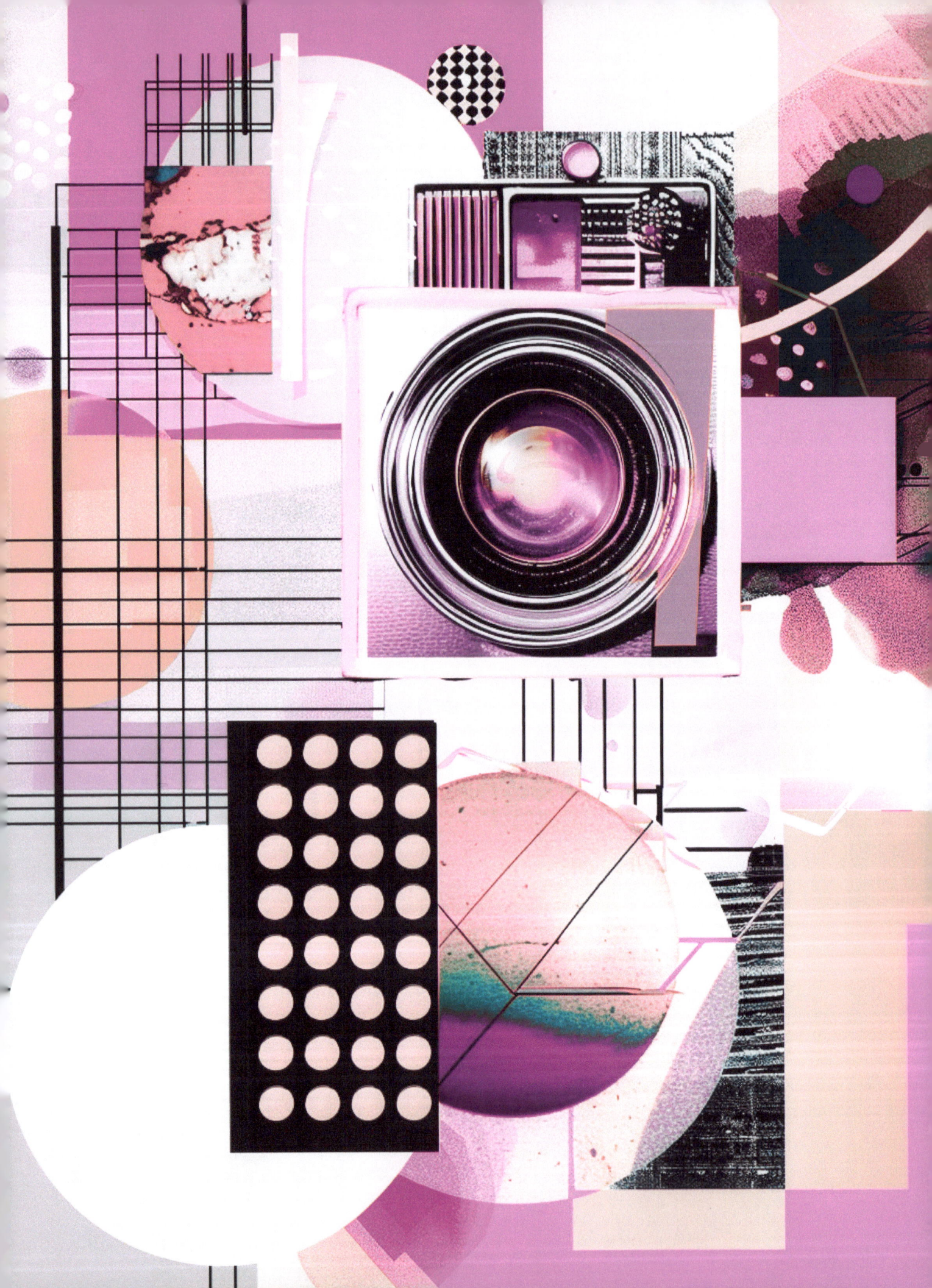

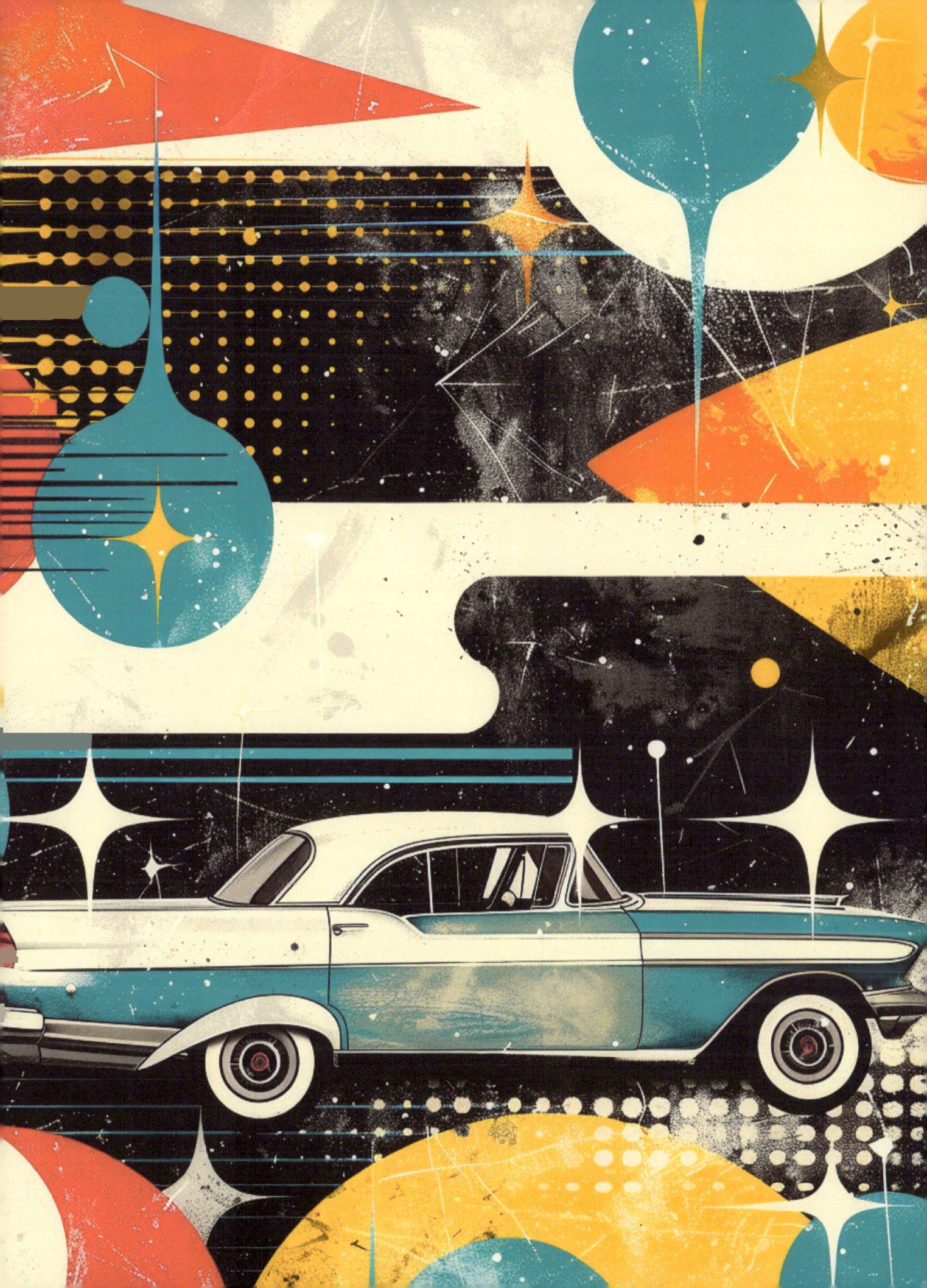

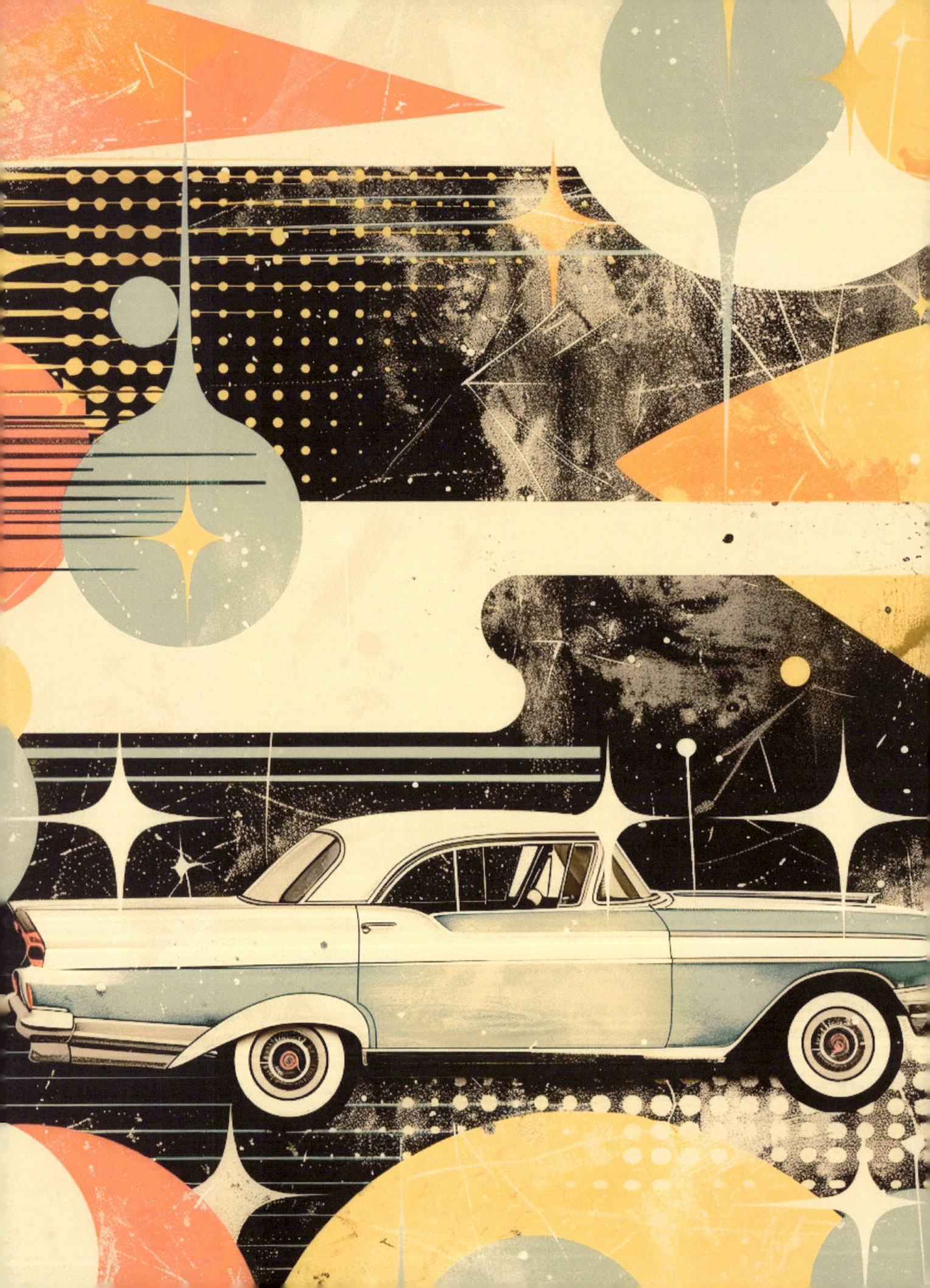

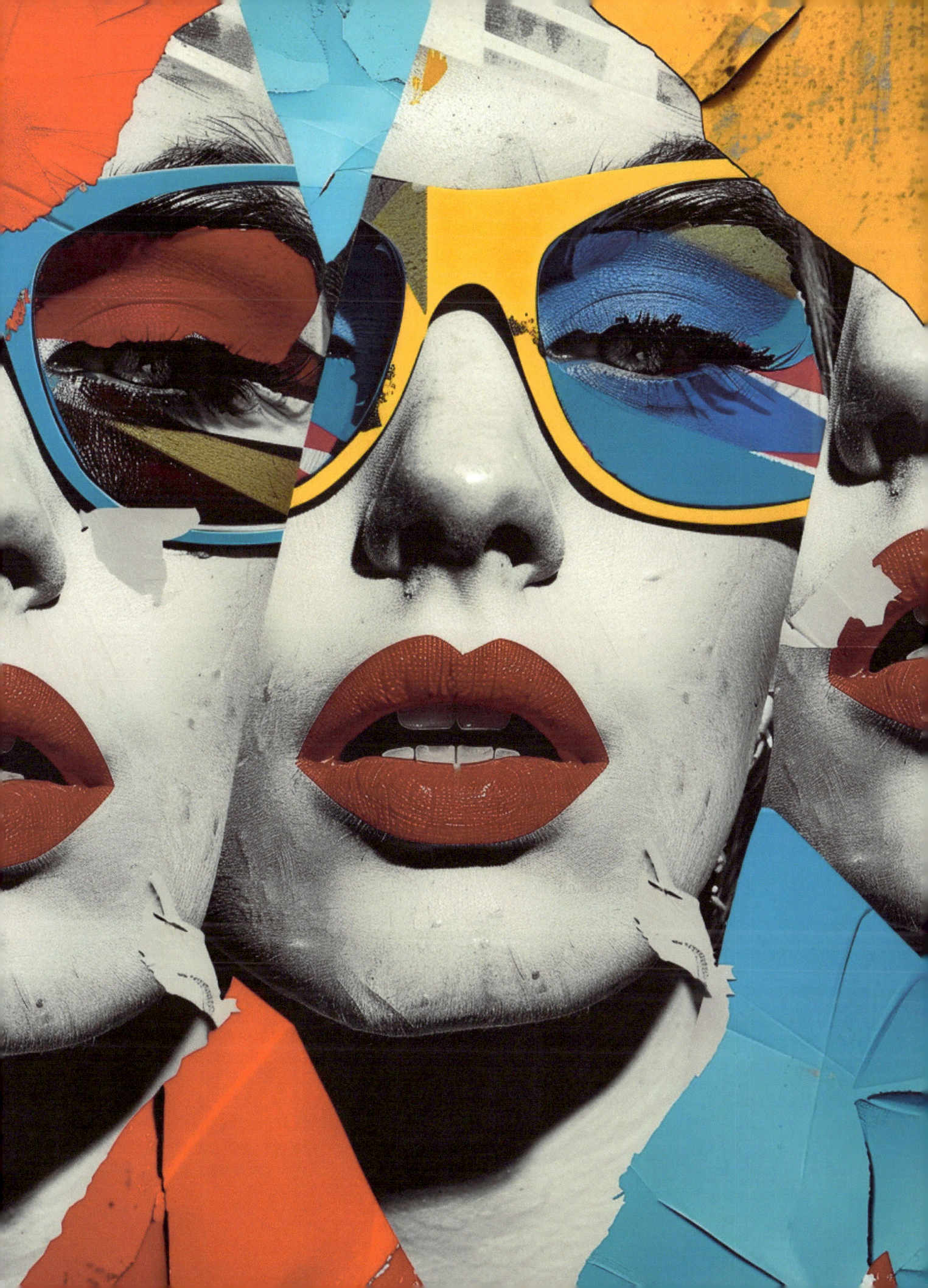

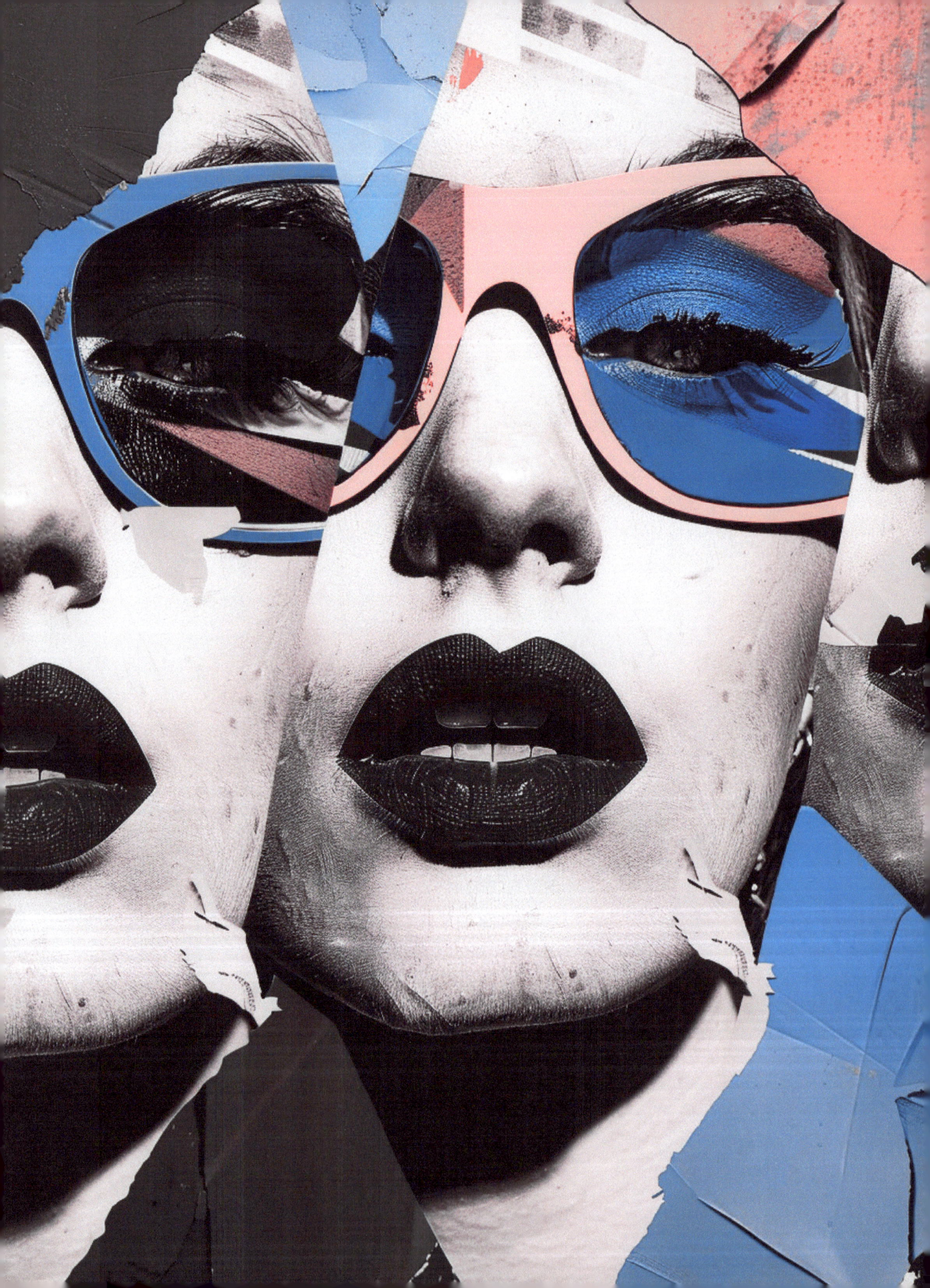

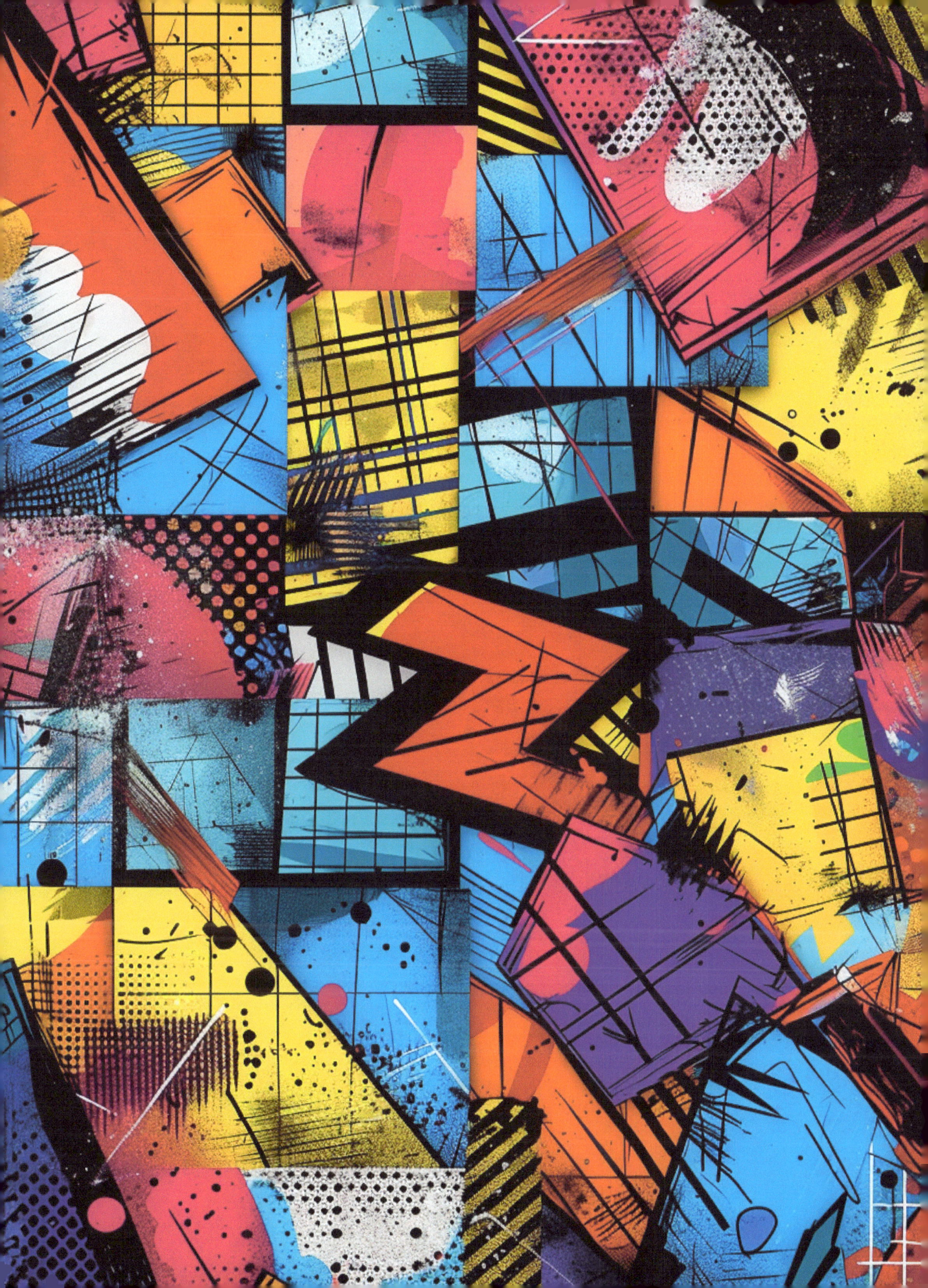

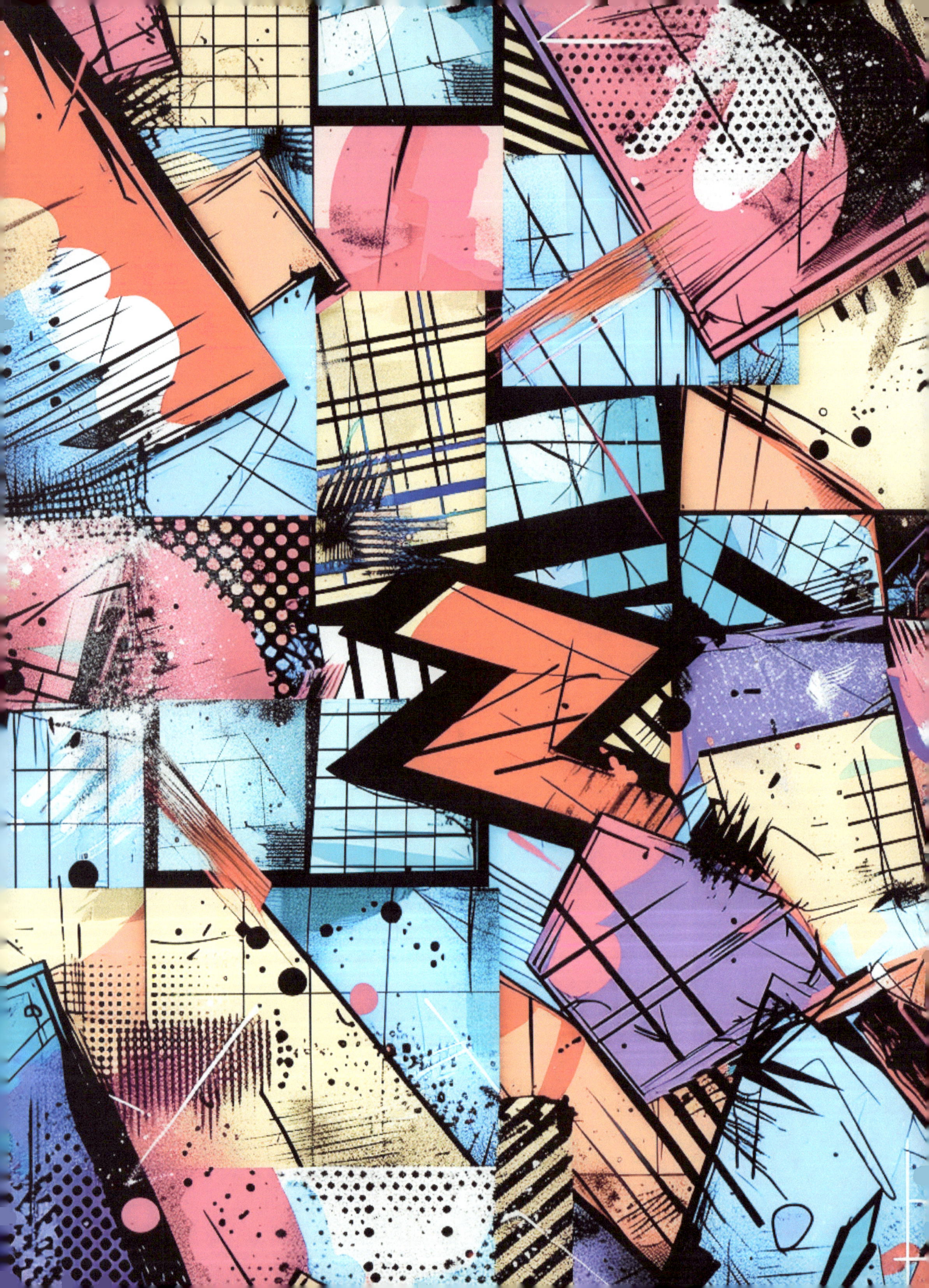

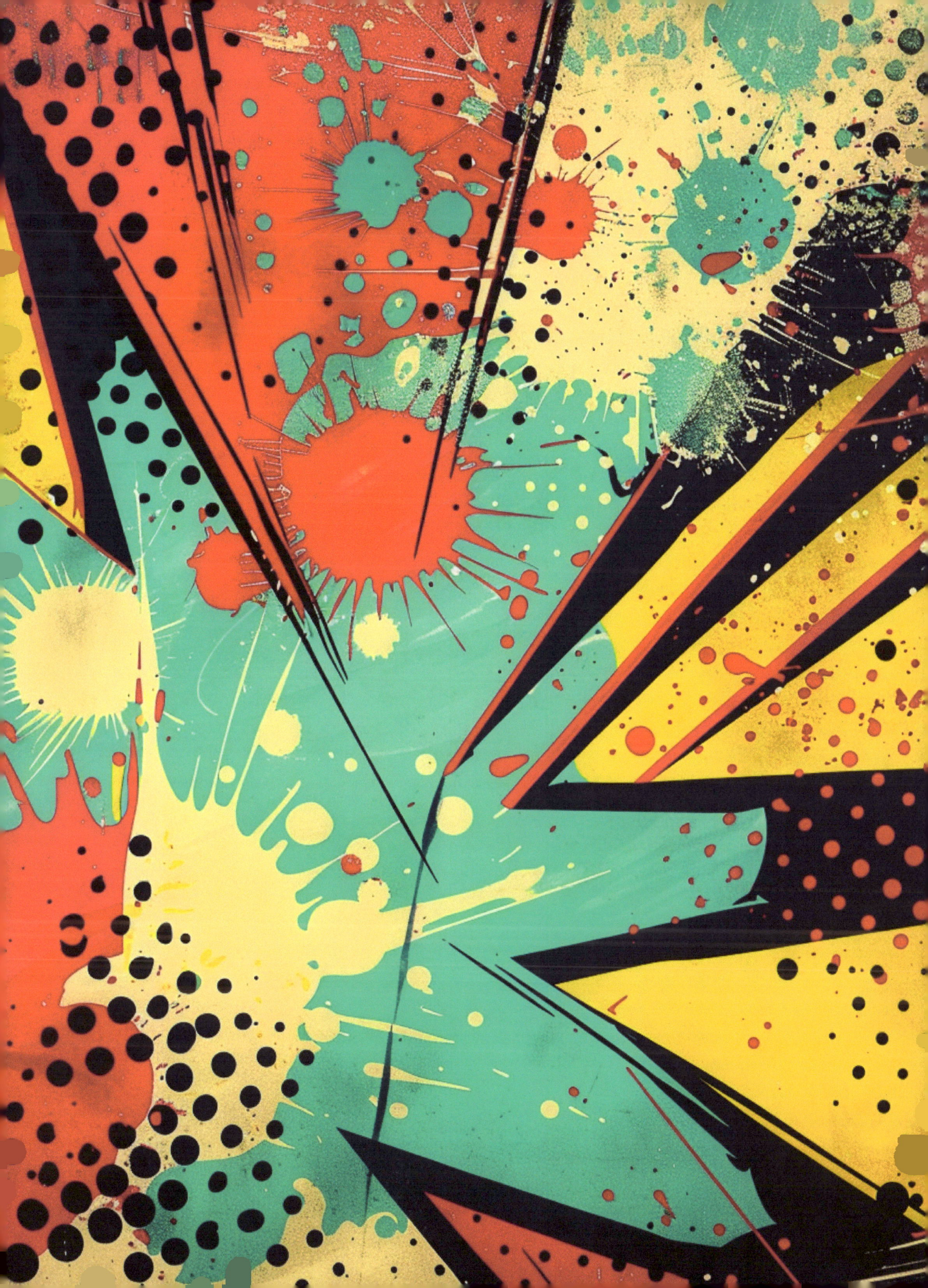

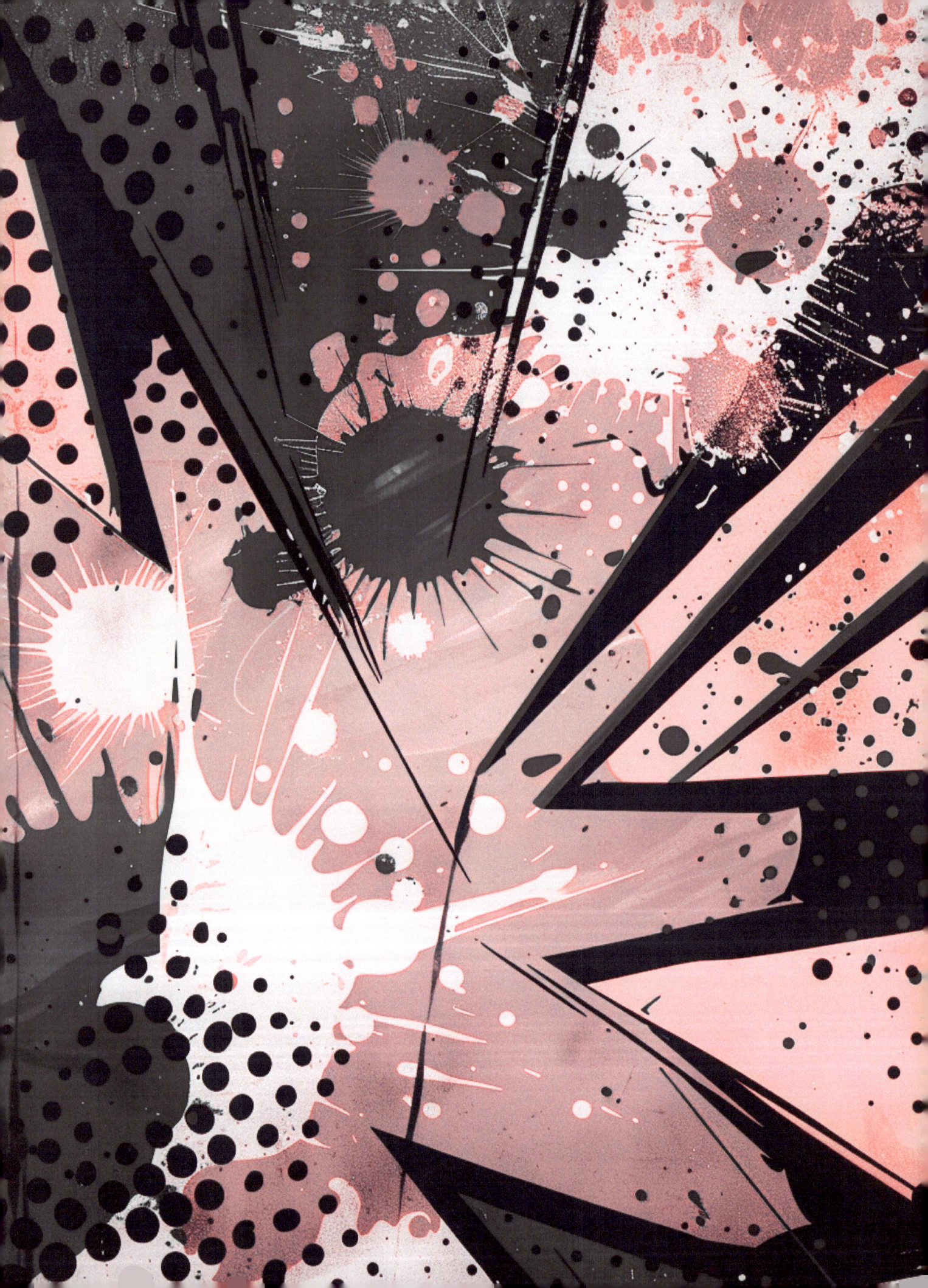

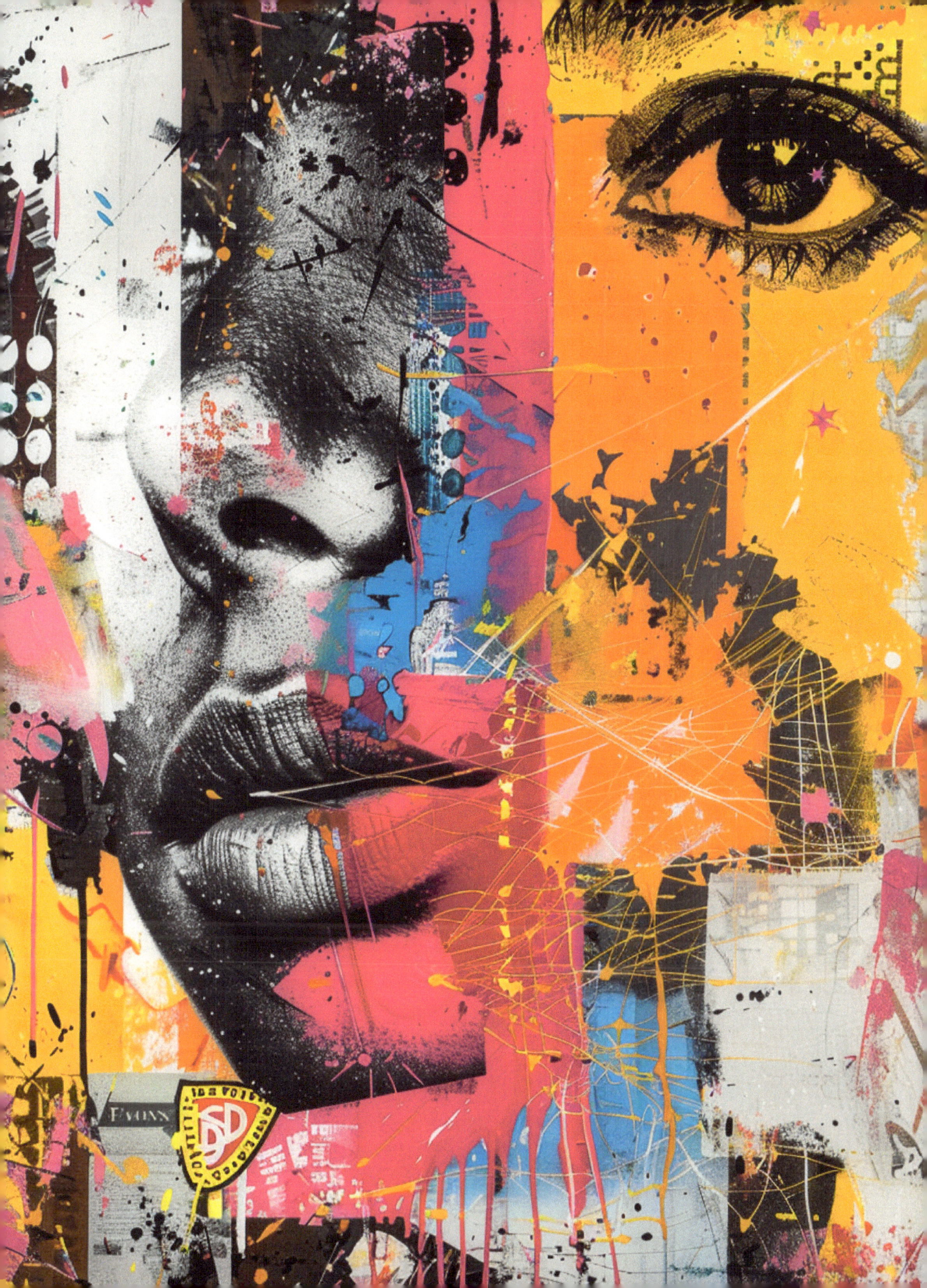

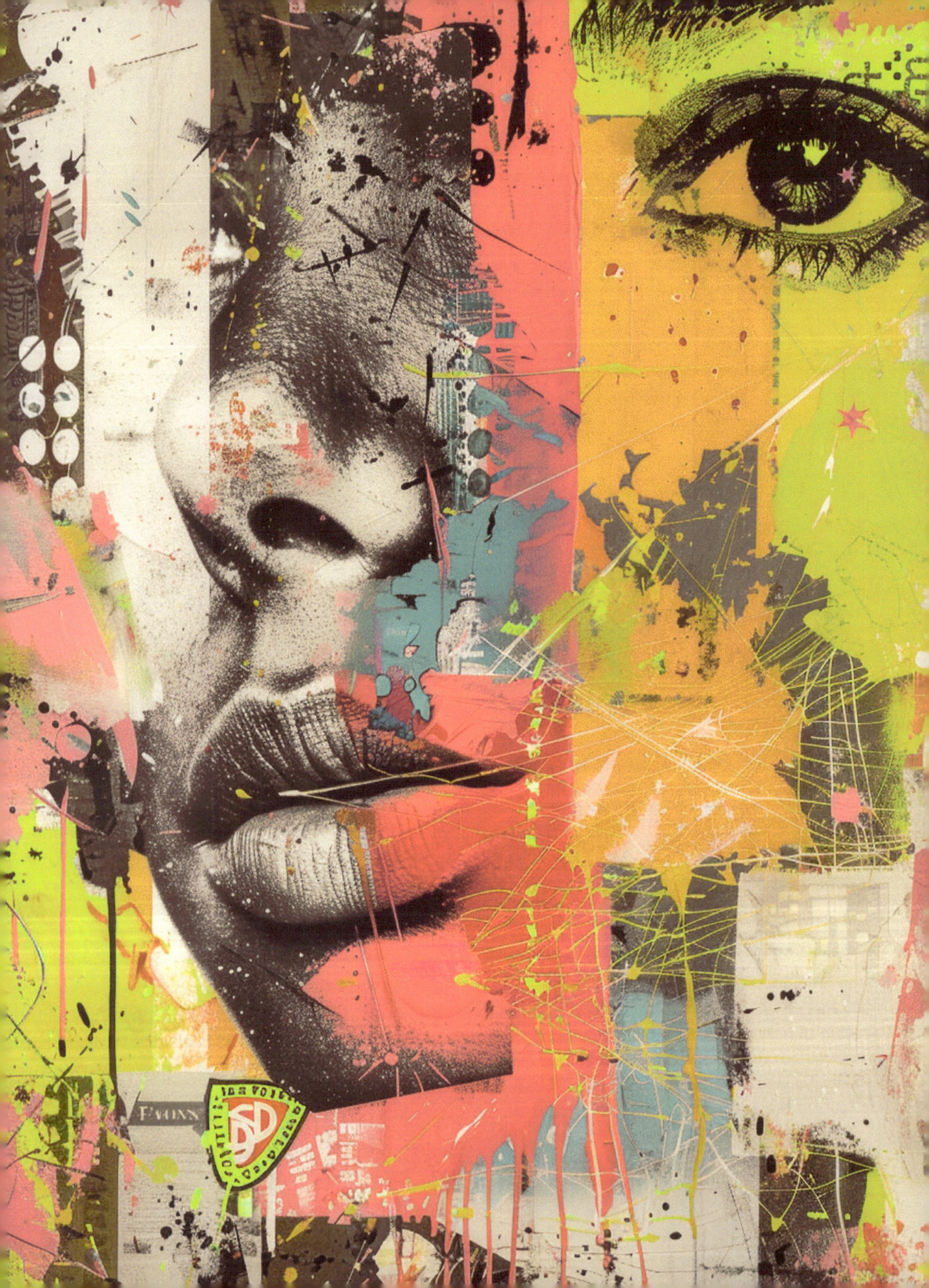

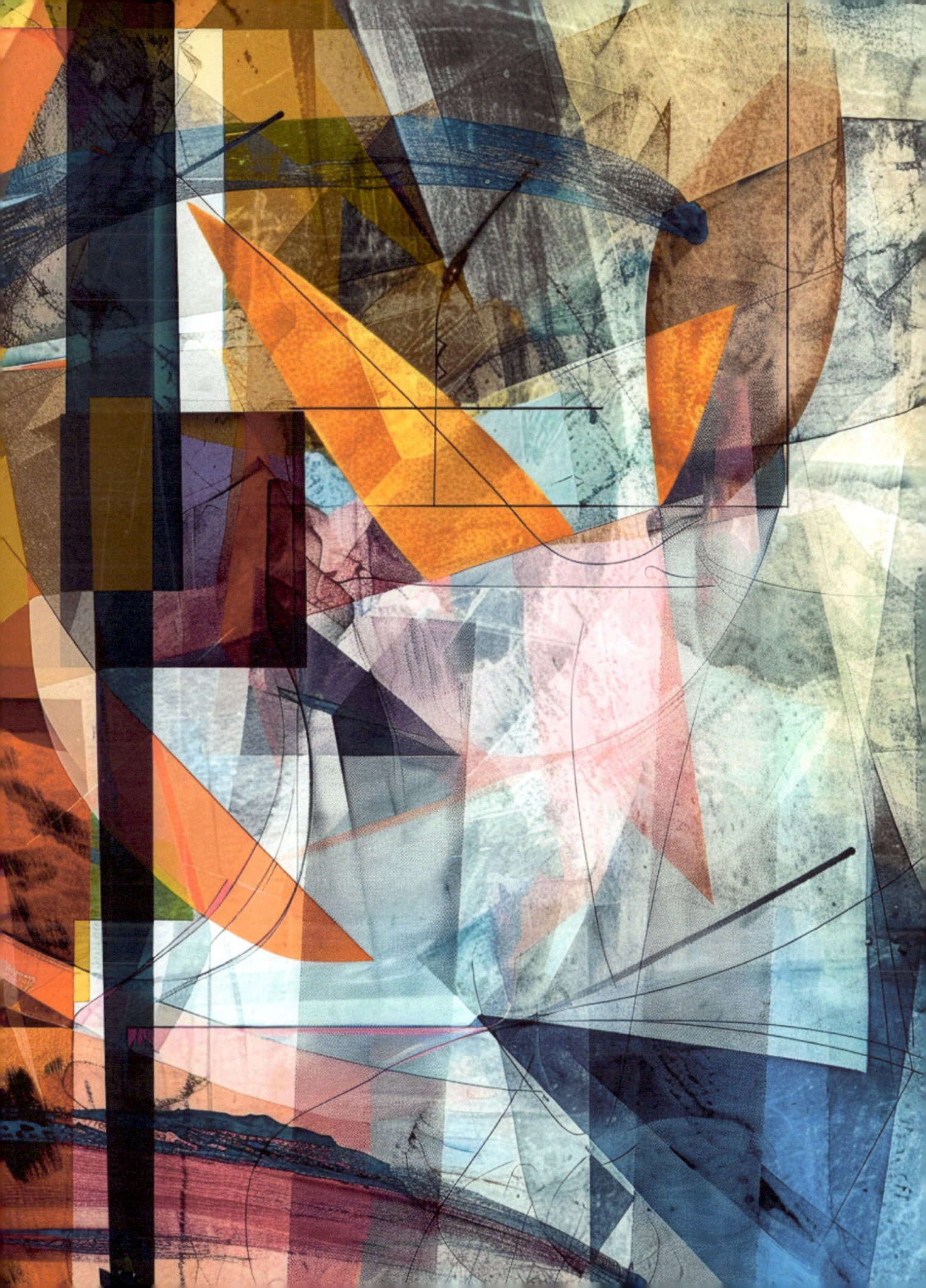

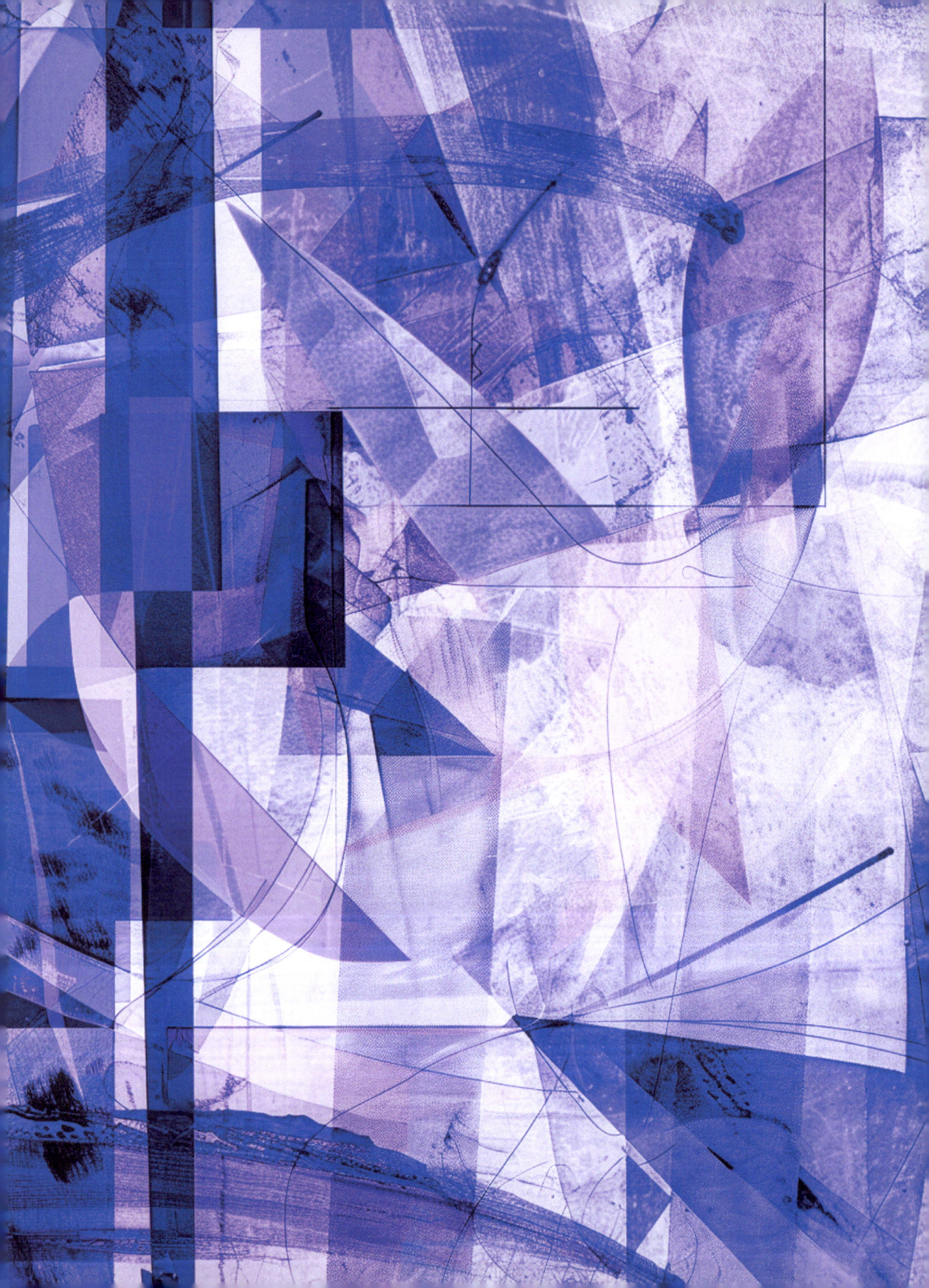

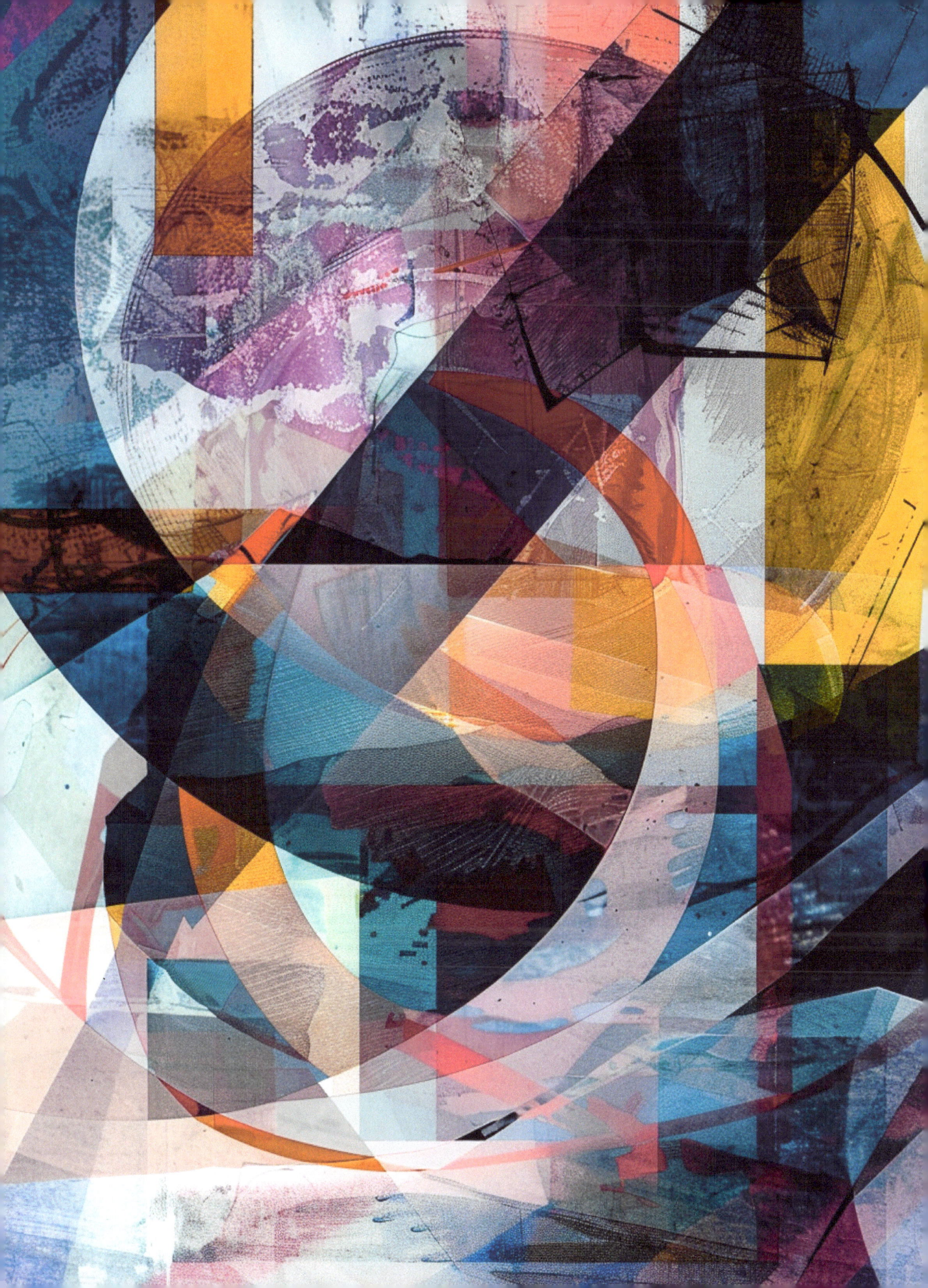

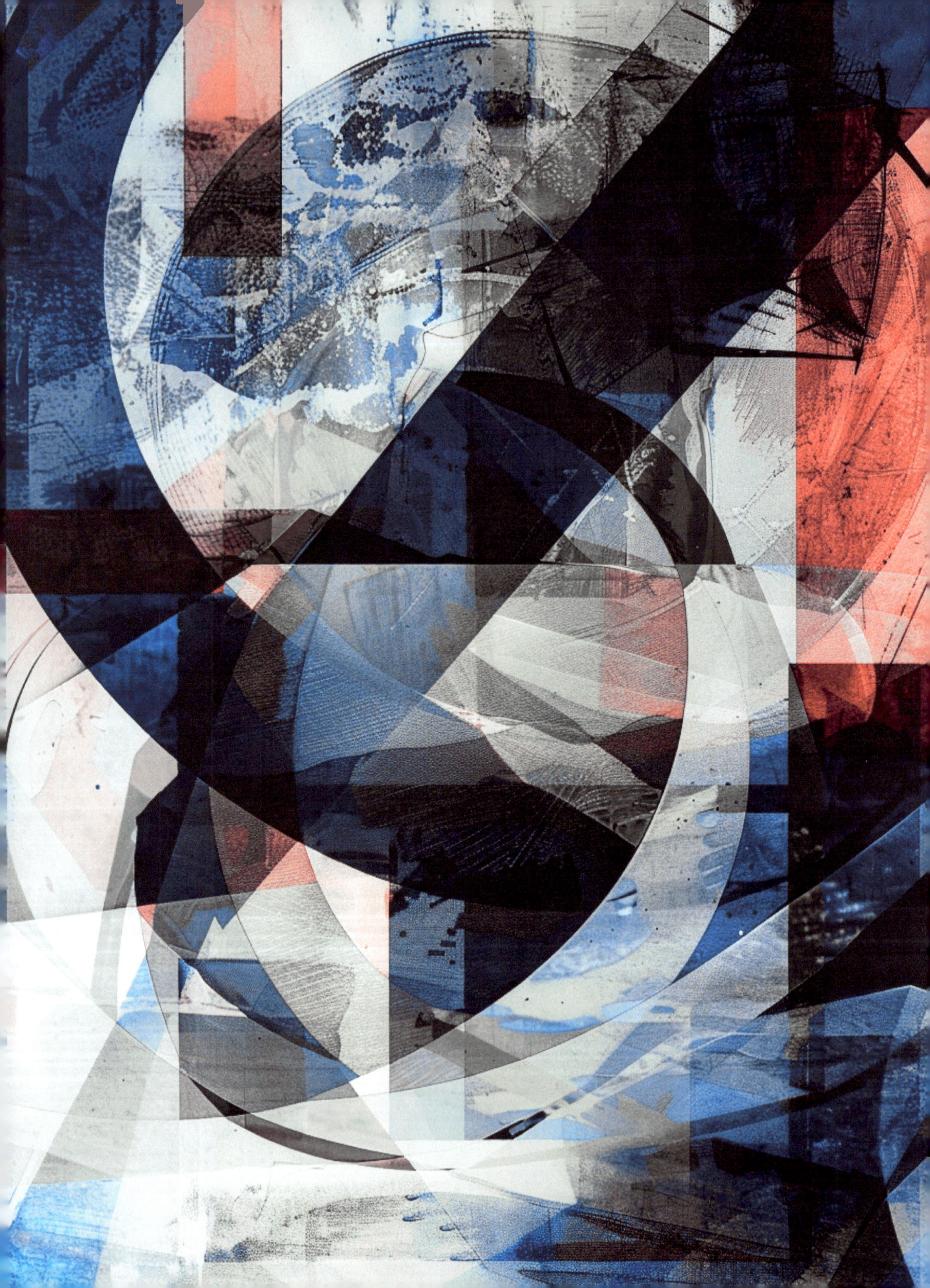

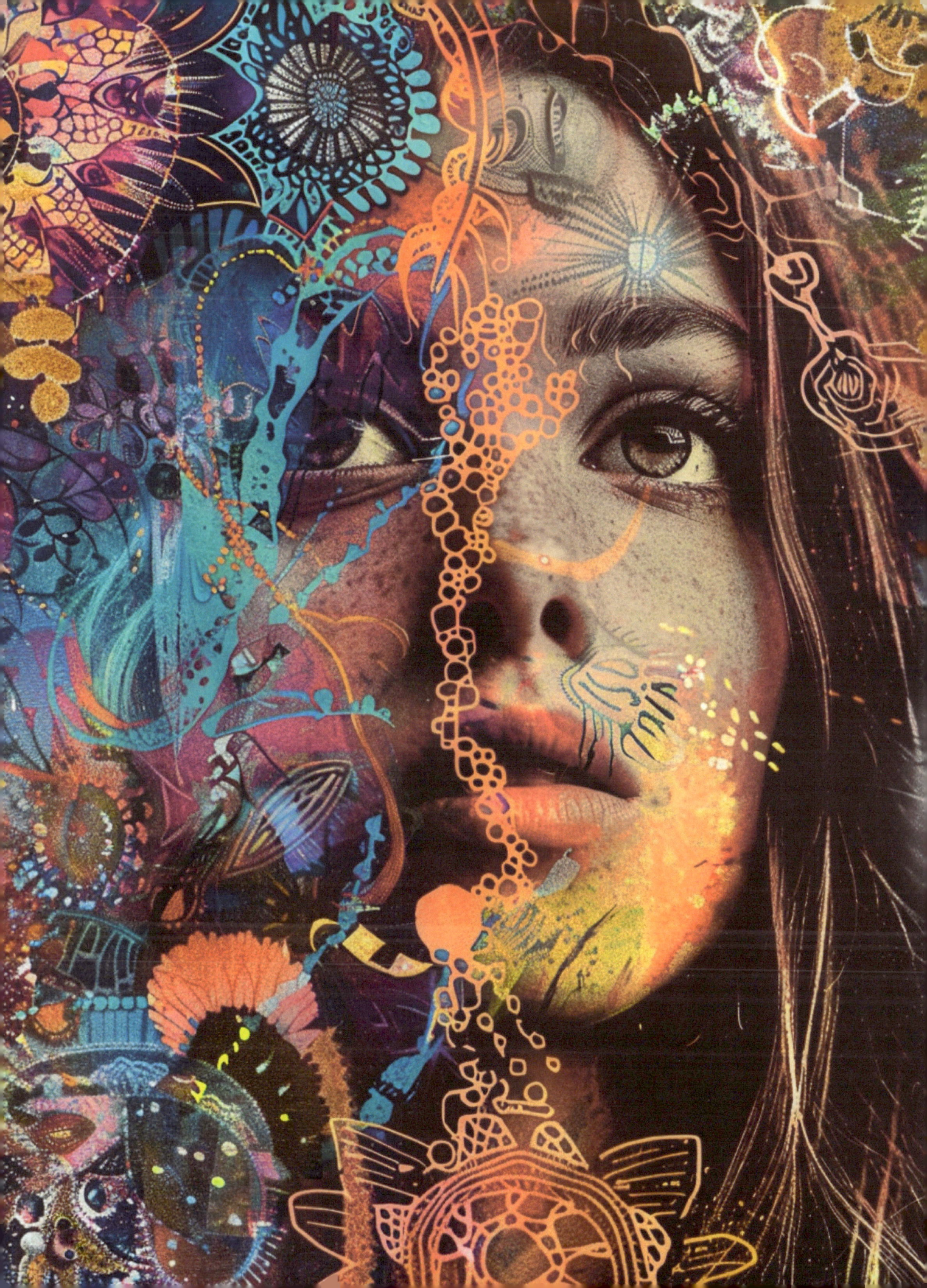

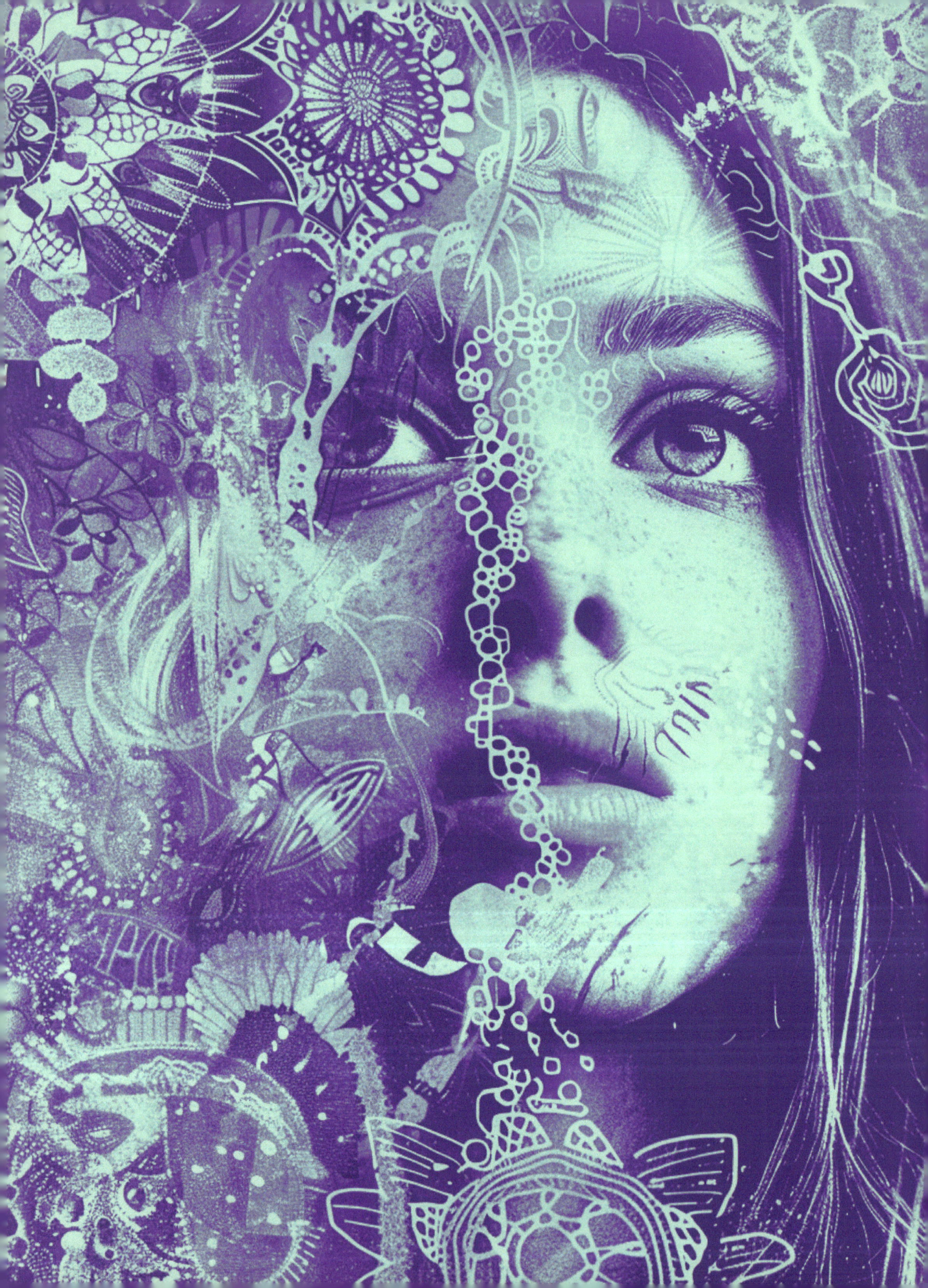

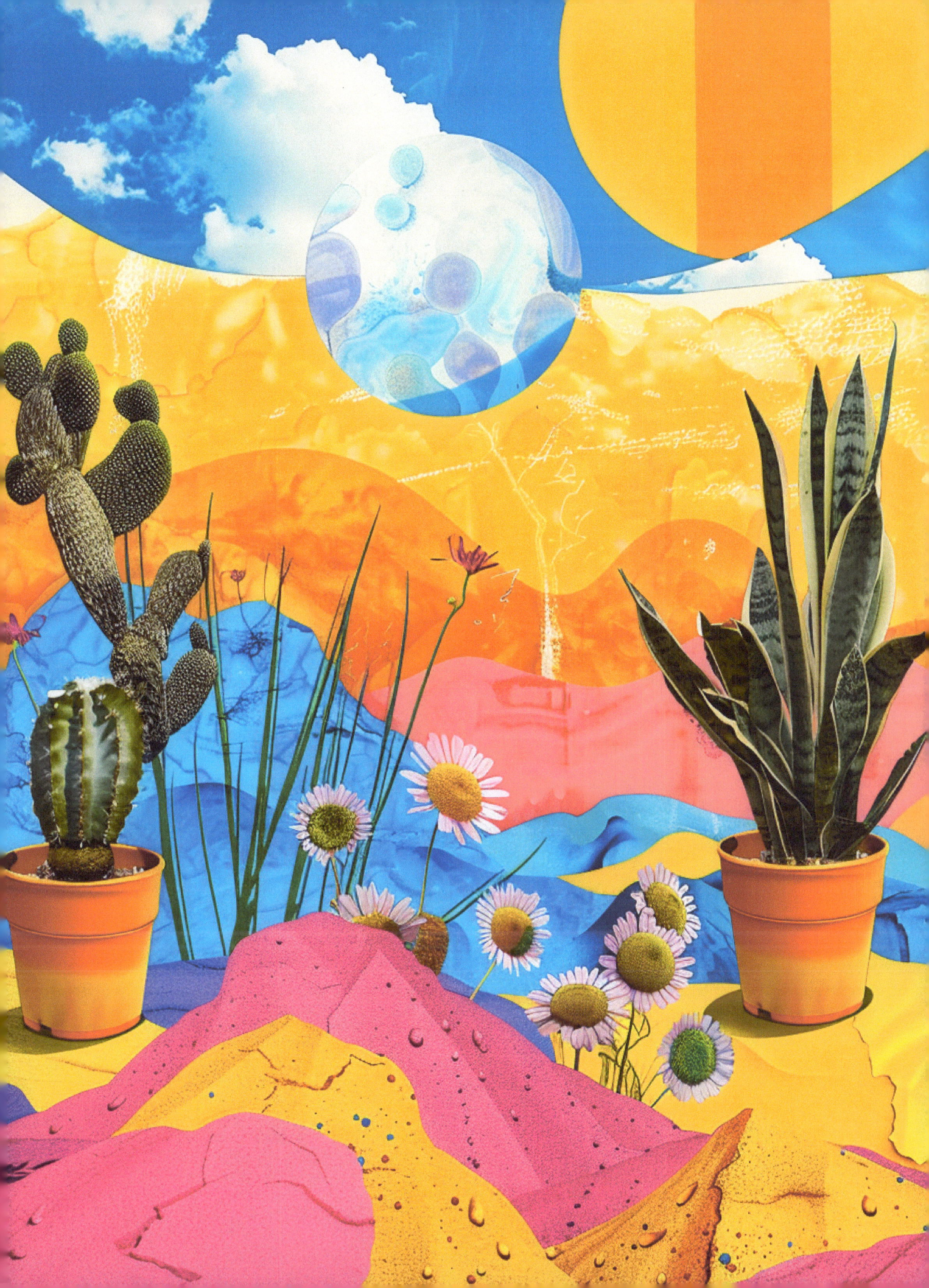

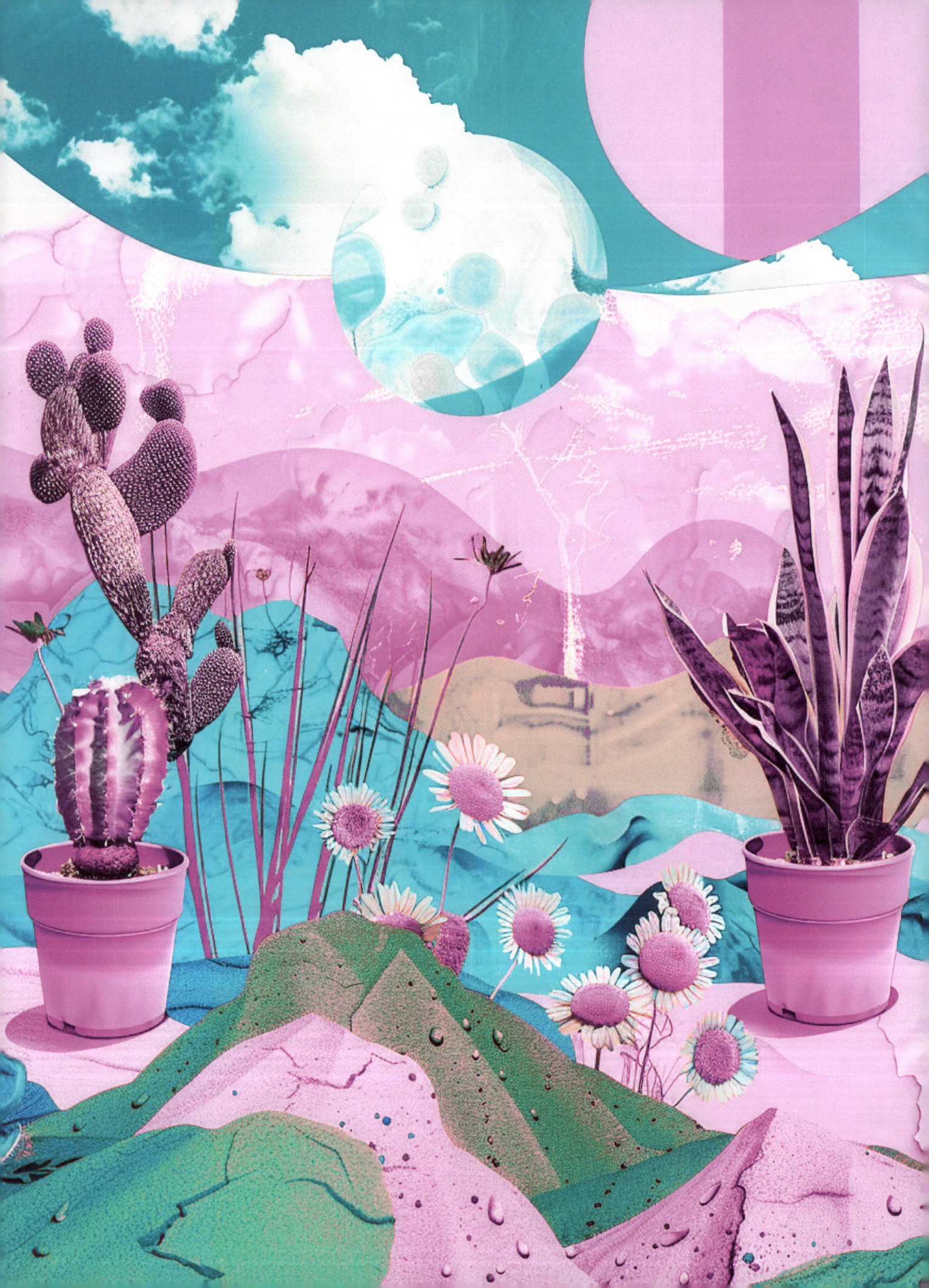

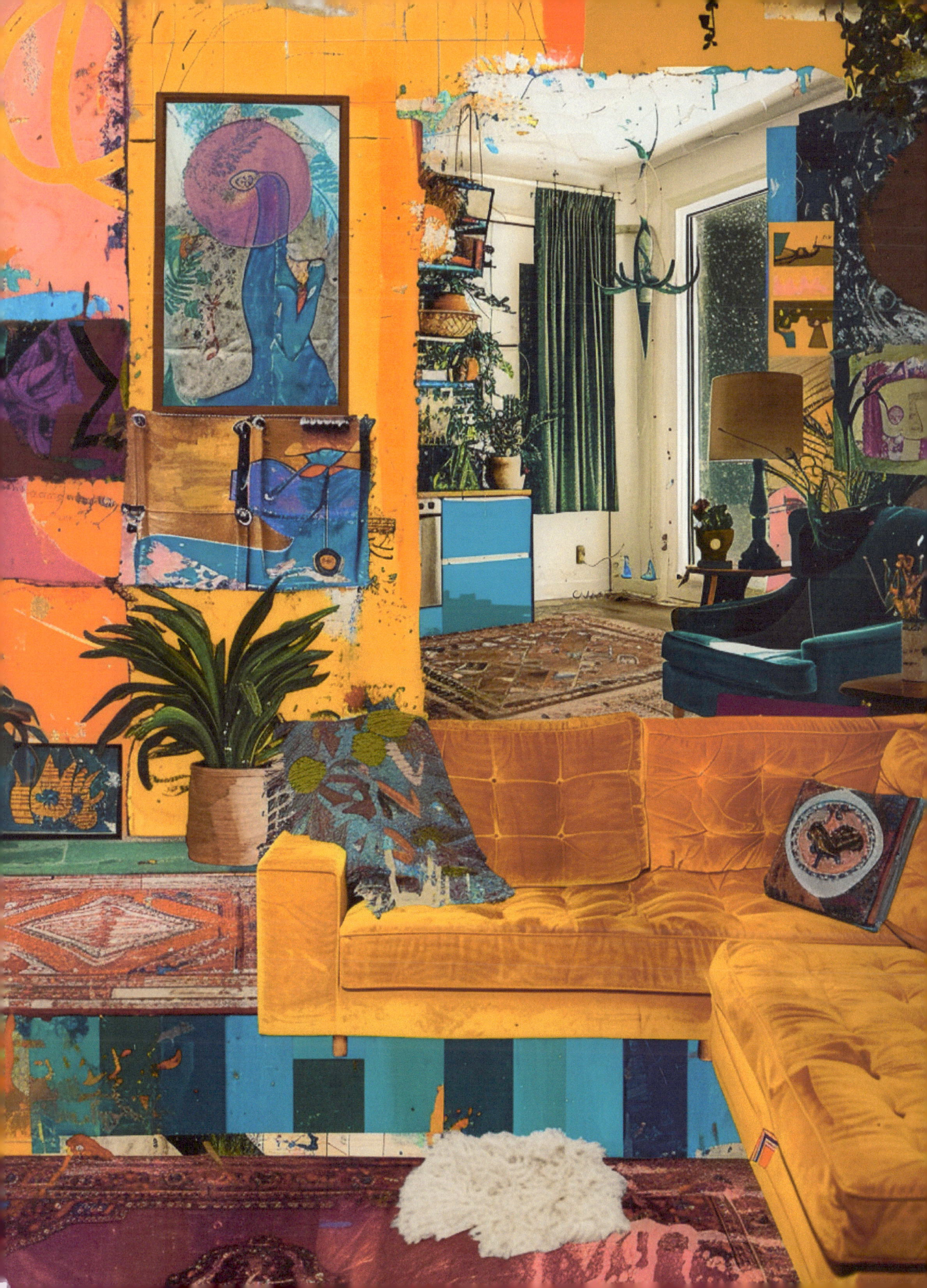

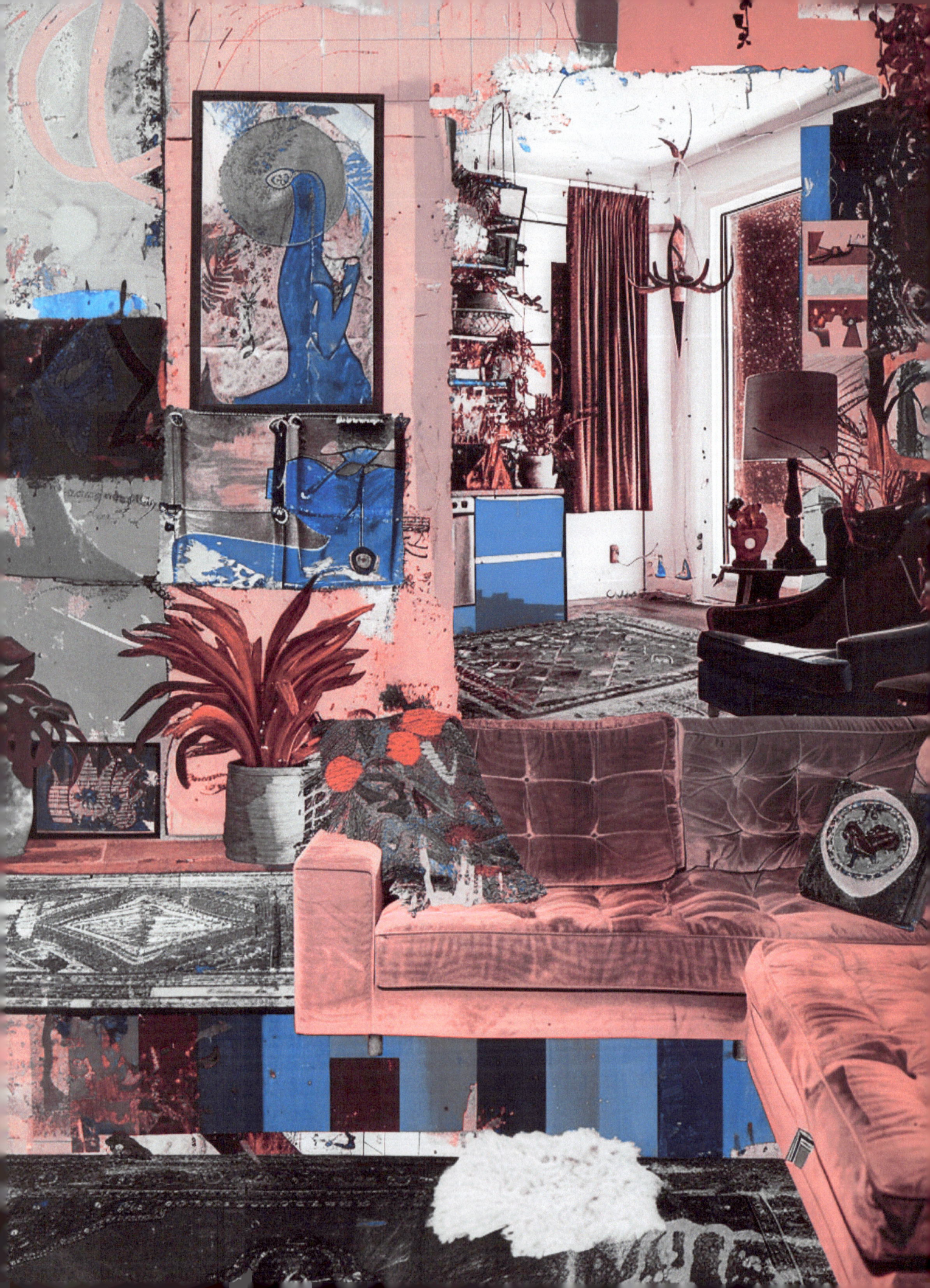